DEVIL'S GALLOP

DEVIL'S GALLOP

Trips into Scotland's Dark and Bloody Past

Douglas Skelton

MAINSTREAM
PUBLISHING

EDINBURGH AND LONDON

First published in Great Britain in 2001 by
MAINSTREAM PUBLISHING COMPANY (EDINBURGH) LTD
7 Albany Street
Edinburgh EH1 3UG

ISBN 1 84018 409 4

A catalogue record for this book is available
from the British Library

Typeset in Baskerville and Van Dijck
Printed and bound in Great Britain by
Cox and Wyman Ltd

Contents

Acknowledgements

No book can be produced without a great deal of help. Here are the people who have helped me:

Thank you to my wife Margaret for planning the trips and packing the picnic basket; Gary McLaughlin, for his advice on the photography; Graham Turnbull, for his help with the technology; John Wilson of Kilwinnet, for the loan of books and other info; Dane Love for the information on Maggie Osborne; Karin Stewart of *Stewart Lucas Hair and Beauty* for battling with the bouffant after the Scottish wind got at it. (It's the first time I've seen a hairdresser use a chair and a whip.) Finally, thanks to Bill Campbell and the staff at Mainstream for their help and patience.

Introduction

The woman in the tourist information centre sounded puzzled. 'You're looking for what?'

'Sawney Beane's cave,' I repeated into the telephone, suddenly feeling very foolish. After all, these people are more used to dealing with enquiries about Rabbie Burns, not the bogeymen of yesteryear. 'He and his family supposedly lived somewhere on the south Ayrshire coast, in a cave.'

'How long ago was this?'

'Oh, centuries ago. They were quite an extended family who operated as a band of robbers and their cave was like Aladdin's cave, if you know what I mean. And they ate people.'

'Ate people?' I heard her voice change then. Up until that point in the conversation she had been attentive and ready to help, but now she saw my query wandering into the realm of Hannibal Lecter and a nice Chianti.

'Well, so the legend goes,' I added quickly, trying to keep my voice light, lest she thought I was the kind of person who would bid at an auction for Jeffrey Dahmer's fridge.

'And you want to find this cave?'

'Well, yes. I'm writing a book, you see, on famous Scottish murderers and I want to do a chapter on Sawney Beane. So I thought I'd like to visit his cave, just to get a feel for it, you know?'

'A feel for eating people, you mean?' I thought I could hear a smile in her voice, but I wasn't sure. It's a reaction I've grown used to over the years whenever I express my interest in the darker side of history. Most people either take an involuntary step backwards, while thinking of rushing home to lock up their daughters – or smile indulgently, while thinking of rushing home to lock up their daughters.

The tourist information lady could not help me, although someone in her office had heard of the villainous Beane clan and believed the cave was reputed to be somewhere near Ballantrae.

That was ten years ago. The Sawney Beane chapter never made it into *Blood on the Thistle*, my book on famous Scottish murders. However, the trip from Glasgow to Ballantrae that day – and in many subsequent forays down the West Coast – yielded up more grisly nuggets than just Scotland's own family of cannibal underground dwellers. Meanwhile, other journeys all over Scotland provided further material on this small country's bloody past in fact and legend.

Someone once said that Scotland is becoming one vast theme park and I see nothing particularly wrong with that. As long as the tourist trade creates employment and generates income, then there is no reason why we should not capitalise on our past. The problem is, we don't do it enough. We have a rich and fascinating history that is there to be merchandised and – dare I say it? Yes, I dare – EXPLOITED. There is more to Scotland than tartan and shortbread, more than Burns and bagpipes. The 1995 movies *Braveheart* and *Rob Roy* showed there is an international interest in our past. As long as it's bloody.

Glencoe and Culloden continue to draw visitors. One of the West Coast's most popular tourist attractions is Inveraray Jail, with its tales of crime and punishment. When people visit our castles, the first thing many want to see are the dungeons. Meanwhile, lines of visitors gawp at instruments of torture and execution in museums. Not long ago I was part of an appreciative crowd in Culzean Castle gardens, watching members of a historical society knocking lumps out of each other in hand-to-hand combat. I heard many different languages spoken that day, but all of them loved the spectacle. We all enjoy a bit of violence – as long as no one actually gets hurt, of course.

But what do guidebooks to castles spend much of their precious space discussing? Architecture and furniture, that's what. It's all very interesting but it's not what I and many others have come to see. It's not very PC to admit it, but when I tour Holyrood Palace I don't want to know about a seventeenth-century sideboard, I want to see the spot where Mary Stuart's wee Italian chum Rizzio was murdered. When I go on a tour of Glasgow, I don't care which buildings Alexander

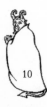

DEVIL'S GALLOP

'Greek' Thomson designed, I want to see where the public gallows were once situated.

Of course, there are now tours in Edinburgh and Glasgow specialising in ghosts and gristle and what jolly fun they are too. However, despite having written about more modern horrors, I have no desire to go the Hollywood route, where guides show you the hotel in which John Belushi overdosed and other such scandals. No, let us stick to past horrors, which have become less distasteful with the passing of centuries.

So in the following chapters you will find tours a traveller could take if he or she was of a mind to delve into the darkness of the past. In the main, I've stuck to places where the visitor can actually see something connected to the relevant story. We are fortunate in this country that we have so many sites dotting the landscape that are tangible reminders of the past. It is possible to stand on the very flagstones where Robert the Bruce and William Wallace once walked; in the rooms where Mary Queen of Scots plotted; the corridors where the Stuart kings politicked; the countryside where countless soldiers fought, died and committed atrocities. All we need is a little imagination and we can be back there with them.

This is not a comprehensive list of Scottish sites, or even a full list of events that took place at each of those mentioned. I've selected stories that appealed to me, and rejected others because they didn't or because I had only so much space at my disposal. If you have a favourite tale that does not appear then it is possible that I've never heard it.

But before we begin, a word of warning. I am not a historian. I have not researched these stories endlessly to establish whether they are true. In fact, generally I don't give a tinker's cuss whether they are true or not. For me, all that matters is the story – as they say in *The Man Who Shot Liberty Vallance*: 'When the fact becomes legend, print the legend'.

Each trip begins in Glasgow because every journey has to start somewhere.

CANNIBAL RUN

FENWICK – DUNDONALD –
MONKTON – AUCHINCRUIVE –
AYR – DUNURE – CULZEAN –
MAYBOLE – TURNBERRY –
GIRVAN – LENDALFOOT –
BALLANTRAE

ONE

Holy War

Ayrshire is Scotland's Holiday Country. At least, that's what it says on the road signs, even though the sandy attractions of Ayr, Troon and Girvan were superseded in Scottish affections long ago by the sultry charms of the various Costas – Brava, Blanca and Bloody Fortune. Nowadays perhaps the allure of Florida, Cyprus and Turkey attract more Caledonian cash per year than these small seaside towns. But 20 or 30 years ago Ayrshire really was Scotland's Holiday Country. Holidaymakers made their way west by the thousand, desperate for some sun, sea and sand. And this being Scotland, they mostly found just the sea and sand.

Even I remember making the great trek to Saltcoats, and I'm not exactly of an age when I need someone else to chew my food. Later, I was taken to Butlin's at Ayr, where I learned such invaluable skills as being able to spot a glamorous granny at 40 feet, and how to jam as many items as possible into a matchbox. (I found it was easier when you took the matches out.)

Time was, the gateway to Ayrshire from Glasgow was the old A77, running through the south side of the city, taking in parts of Newton Mearns and Whitecraigs, areas where a deep breath of air brought with it the unmistakeable whiff of money. The people here are by no means Beverly Hills rich, of course, but most of them are decidedly comfortable. For decades spiky-haired scallywags pressed their noses up against the windows of a blue Western Scottish bus (this was in the days when Stagecoach was merely a classic John Wayne movie) to gaze in awe at the neat houses and well-tended gardens and to wonder how anyone could live in such opulence. For years, the owners of those desirable properties complained about the levels of traffic, which comprised not only motor cars but also lorries and the aforementioned

DEVIL'S GALLOP

buses, that choked the air with diesel fumes. They complained and griped and petitioned until finally money was found to build a new road which would take the traffic from the M8 to Ayrshire, by-passing the residential areas.

Of course, that wasn't the end of it. The new M77 was to slice off part of a rambling parkland, cut through greenfield sites and come very near to some housing schemes, whose tenants were none too chuffed at the thought of all that pollution wafting into their children's lungs. So they complained and they griped and they petitioned but the government of the day ignored them. The government also ignored a group of environmental activists – or troublemaking layabouts, as they were officially known – who built a village in the branches of trees destined to be cut down in the name of progress. The tree people became something of a sensation in the area – Scotland not being known for such open defiance of authority – and their camp became a mecca for journalists and dropouts (two groups often difficult to tell apart). You can see the remnants of the wood they called home from the M77, just at the 'off' ramp for Pollok. If you look hard enough, you may even see a plank of wood or a piece of ragged plastic sheeting still hanging from a branch or two.

This wood was said to be the final resting place of a Glasgow criminal, murdered and buried here by some peeved former colleagues where it was thought he would never be found. And he wasn't, despite the eventual use of bulldozers and mechanical diggers to get rid of the campaigners. But the premature burial of some hapless gangster in such places is almost an urban legend in Glasgow. The M8 itself is reputed to be a virtual necropolis, with many a missing mobster said to be propping up its foundations or interred in the cement blocks supporting the Kingston Bridge. When the bridge was recently moved ever so slightly, in a unique operation that attracted worldwide attention, it was suggested that all sorts of cadavers would be popping out of the foundations. But no such impromptu disinterment took place.

However, such comparatively recent foul play was of no interest to me in this trip. I was heading to Ayrshire in pursuit of older, darker horrors. My journey took me to castles both ruined and still in use, to churchyards large and small, to roadside stones commemorating murder and death at sea, to small towns with dark tales to tell and quiet beaches which, if legend is to be believed, once ran red with blood thanks to a family who when they had you for dinner, they HAD you for dinner.

My first step on the Cannibal Run was to make my way onto the M8. This vast motorway slices through the centre of the city – not to mention central Scotland – like a deep wound, stitching Edinburgh in the east to Greenock in the west. Travellers might also cross the Kingston Bridge – the busiest road bridge in Europe, they say, and anyone who has been stuck in traffic jams at peak hours can well believe it.

Heading west, I turned off at signs for Kilmarnock and Prestwick Airport. This is the M77 and a word of warning is needed here – this may be a motorway, but the speed limit for much of its length is 50 mph. Regular patrols of traffic cops can be spotted, either in motion or lurking in special bays at the side of the road. They are known as 'T' or 'Tango' Division in Strathclyde and if they catch you doing a David Coulthard then you will indeed know you have been Tangoed.

Once past the outskirts of the city, the multi-laned motorway became a two-lane blacktop and I was once more following the route of the old A77. Eventually, this opened up into a four-lane road, and some way on I took the turn-off for Fenwick, the village that gives its name to the vast moorland stretching to Eaglesham in the north and Strathaven in the east. It was in the churchyard of the handsomely white-painted kirk that I found the graves of a number of martyrs to a religious cause that brought death to thousands during the seventeenth century. And to understand just why, I must give you a short history lesson. Settle back now, this may take some time.

The Highlands had the Jacobites. The Lowlands had the Covenanters. Although diametrically on opposite sides of the religious divide, at different times they both threatened the authority of kings and governments and both were quite ruthlessly hunted down by the authorities.

There were Covenanters as far back as 1557, only back then they were known as Supplicants. They were fiercely opposed to any form of anglicisation of Scottish Presbyterianism, a form of Christianity in

which there aren't many laughs. These po-faced fundamentalists made Oliver Cromwell's boys look like a very merry band indeed and they signed covenants in 1557 and 1581 vowing to uphold Presbyterianism no matter what it took. And just to make sure, they reinforced these vows in 1590 and 1596.

In 1625, Charles I came to the throne and promptly decided that the Scottish Kirk should become Anglican. Bishops would oversee the Church from now on, he said, and they would be answerable to him. The Supplicants took none too kindly to this notion, believing that their Church should be answerable to no monarch. To them, too, the English religion appeared to be nothing more than Roman Catholicism with a king as Pope. This, together with heavy taxes inflamed many a Scottish heart, for if there was one thing the Scots hated more than attacks on their devotions it was someone dipping into their purse.

In 1638, the General Assembly of Scotland sent Charles's Anglicans home, thus causing the First Bishops' War in 1639. One year later, a new Assembly met and repeated that there would be no incense burning, kneeling or chanting in their services, thank you very much, and they again rejected the English Church. This prompted the cleverly named Second Bishops' War. (For those reading this in Hollywood, this was *Bishops' War 2 – This Time It's Parsonal*.)

Three years later, both English and Scottish Parliaments adopted a Solemn League and Covenant – designed to protect the Church, oppose Roman Catholicism and stick a tongue out at the King. The Supplicants, now officially known as the Covenanters, played for the Parliamentary side against the Royalists during the First Civil War fixtures between 1642 and 1646. It was a Covenanting side who actually captured the King, turning him, and no doubt his spaniels, over to Cromwell's squad when His Royal High-and-Mightyness still refused to accept the Solemn League. Charles, of course, had a close encounter with the headsman's axe, which horrified the Scots. They may have had their differences with him over religion, but he was still their king and didn't deserve the chop off the old block. It wasn't long before the Covenanters began to fear Cromwell's growing power. Eventually they saw him as the devil's disciple, something they were wont to do to anyone they dropped from their Christmas card list, and went to war against him, too. They gave their support to Charles II (or *Charles 2 – He's Back and Mad as Hell!*). Chuckie Mark Two had won them over when he cleverly agreed to the Solemn League *and* the Covenant. This, however, all came unstuck at Dunbar in 1650 (see Border Raid).

Charles did finally win his throne in 1660, but only because Cromwell had died two years previously and the Parliamentarians had felt the lack of his steady hand. The new king, despite having sworn to uphold the Covenant, proceeded to persecute his former followers with a vengeance, no doubt recalling that it was they who had handed his dear dead dad over 14 years before. Across south-west Scotland, ministers refused to follow the new order and were forced to give up their parishes. Many went on the road as itinerant preachers, holding conventicles (illegal services held in barns or in secluded glens) and always looking over their shoulders for government troops. All the blood shed up until that point was but a pinprick compared to the rivers that would follow. For these were the so-called 'Killing Times', when government troops roamed the fields and forests of Ayrshire and Galloway, slaughtering anyone who refused to bend a knee to the King's version of religion.

There is hardly a kirkyard in Ayrshire without some mention of a Covenanter or two, and Fenwick has a number of them. Each of the graves is clearly marked and it's amazing what you learn by reading headstones. A Peter Gemmell, for instance, was 'shot to death by [Lieutenant Robert] Nisbet and his party 1685 for bearing his faithful testimony to the cause of Christ, aged 21 years'. The bloodthirsty redcoats 'cut his prayers short' and 'even his dying groans were made their sport'.

Meanwhile, the inscription writers gave doggerel a bad name with their description of the brutal death of James White – who, we learn, was shot to death at Little Blackwood by Peter Ingles and his party in 1685. White's head was hacked from his body and later Ingles paraded it before the garrison at Newmilns, allowing his men to use it as a football. The inscription reads:

> This martyr was by Peter Ingles shot,
> by birth a tyger rather than a Scot,

DEVIL'S GALLOP

> Who, that his monstrous extract might be seen,
> Cut off his head and kick't it o'er the green.
> Thus was that head which was to wear a crown,
> A football made by a profane dragoon.

There are memorials to Covenanters not actually buried in Fenwick. One is Reverend William Guthrie who was the first minister of Fenwick Parish (the church here was built in 1643). He was ejected by prelatic persecution (which doesn't half make your eyes water) in 1664 and died one year later. He is actually buried in Brechin but the villagers erected this stone in 1854. Others who are here in spirit, if not actually in bodily remains, are: Robert Buntine (or Bunton) – executed in Glasgow and James Blackwood – put to death in Irvine (more on him later), both in 1666. Both men had been captured during the short-lived Pentland Rising.

Captain John Paton is also memorialised. He went to the gallows in Edinburgh's Grassmarket in 1684 and his mortal remains:

> sleep amid the dust of kindred martyrs in the Greyfriars Churchyard, Edinburgh. He fought for his country on the continent and for his religion at Pentland, Drumclog and Bothwell. His heroic conduct truly evinced the gallant officer, brave soldier and true patriot in social and domestic life. He was an ornament, a pious Christian, and a faithful witness for the truth in opposition to the encroachments of tyrannical and despotic power in Church and State.

Which is all very laudable, but could he walk, talk and chew gum all at the same time?

In actual fact, Paton was a mercenary who returned to his homeland to fight on the Roundhead side at Marston Moor and against Montrose in Scotland, when the tragic Marquis took the Stuart cause onto battlefields all over Scotland. Paton later fought at Dunbar for the Covenanters against Cromwell, which eventually led him into the doomed Pentland Rising. At Rullion Green, three dragoons tried to capture him but he killed one and told the others to inform their master, General Tam Dalyell, that he would 'not be supping with him tonight'. Paton spent the next 17 years a hunted man until the Covenanter cause was crushed at Bothwell Bridge.

When he was finally captured, his companions wanted to make a fight of it but Paton supposedly told them: 'I am weary of life, being hunted from place to place. I am not afraid to die.'

General Dalyell pleaded with the King for mercy but on 9 May 1684 Robert Paton, now a colonel, was hanged.

According to another headstone, 'the dust' of John Fergushill and George Woodburn lie in the Fenwick dirt. They were shot by Nisbet and his party in 1685. This would be the same wild bunch that did in Peter Gemmell. They were clearly very busy that year. Government troops displayed a marked tendency to shoot anyone they thought to be a 'whig'. Their suspicions could have been aroused simply by finding someone reading the Bible.

Also worth having a look at is the nice set of jougs hanging from the exterior wall of the church. These are the Scottish equivalent of the stocks, much beloved in the sixteenth century by the leaders of the Kirk, who would condemn members of their parish to be chained up by the neck in this contraption for whatever transgression they thought had been committed. A woman could be chained up for enjoying the pleasures of the flesh somewhat too freely. You could also be sent to the jougs for slander, for not going to church, or for working on the Sabbath.

TWO

Birth of a Hero

A yrshire is, of course, the birthplace of Robert Burns, Scotland's national poet and perhaps her most famous son. (Wherever he broke wind is marked by some memorial or other.) But the county does its level best to lay claim to two other notable Scots better known for their prowess with edged weapons than the pen. One is Robert the Bruce, who we shall come to later in this trip. The other is William Wallace.

As I left Fenwick and turned left, back onto the A77, I almost immediately came to signs for Kilmarnock and it was in a suburb of this town that some local writers and historians say William Wallace was born. I did not visit the site, as there is nothing to see, but it is worth considering the claims.

For centuries it was believed that Wallace, the man who would later become Guardian of Scotland and would give the English King Edward Plantagenet a bloody nose at Stirling Bridge, was born at Elderslie in Renfrewshire. The problem is, much of what we know about William Wallace – and there is not really that much – comes from the epic verse of Blind Harry the Minstrel, which was an adaptation of a life of Wallace written in Latin by Wallace's chum John Blair. Unfortunately, that manuscript has disappeared, although rumour has it that a copy lies undiscovered in some secret Vatican archive (no doubt alongside the Ark of the Covenant and Shergar).

Blind Harry tells us that William was the son of Sir Malcolm Wallace (a minor noble whose family may originally have come from Wales) but not the exact date of his birth, although most writers place it as somewhere between 1270 and 1274. There were Wallaces all over Ayrshire, including Ellerslie, which lay to the west of Kilmarnock and was in the diocese of the Bishop of Paisley – as was Elderslie. Also in

Ayrshire's favour is the fact that Blind Harry names Wallace's mother as Margaret de Crauford, daughter of the hereditary Sheriff of Ayrshire, whose family home was at Loudoun. Also, when Wallace first went on the run, after an affray in Dundee, it was to Ayrshire that he fled and not Renfrewshire.

On the other hand, Wallace historian David R. Ross has pointed out that on ancient maps, Elderslie was called Ellerslie and the Renfrewshire castle is registered as being in the hands of Wallaces from about 1390. Confused? Welcome to Scottish history.

Local tradition has young Wallace in Ayrshire, making himself unpopular with the English. His father was born at Riccarton on the outskirts of Kilmarnock (there is a plaque outside the fire station there, marking his birthplace) and it was while young William was staying with an uncle at the family home that he had an early skirmish with the forces of occupation. He was fishing in the River Irvine when five English soldiers ordered him to hand over the trout he had caught. Wallace refused and the soldiers tried to take the catch by force. Wallace, not being the type to let anyone slap one cheek never mind turning the other, saw red and brained one of the soldiers with his fishing rod. (It must have been a very stout fishing rod. What was he fishing for – marlin?) He then took the soldier's sword and before you could say 'Eddie Plantagenet is a nancy boy', another two had had their chips. The remaining pair made off, presumably in search of a Harry Ramsdens.

With life now too hot for him at home, the young Wallace was forced to leg it to Dundee, where his quick temper soon had him in trouble again (see Rebel March).

DEVIL'S GALLOP

THREE

Dynasty

Heading once again for Ayr on the A77, I kept an eye out for a signpost to turn right onto the B730 towards Dundonald. The small country road has all the usual twists, turns and dips, but it was not long before I saw the ruins of Dundonald Castle standing on a hilltop, dominating the village below. From this vantage point it is easy to see why it was chosen for a fortification. Approaching enemies would be spotted from its ramparts and the elevated position could be defended easily. There has been a camp here since about 500 BC but the first castle was not built until some time between 1142 and 1153.

There is a car park at the foot of the hill, near the visitors' centre. The climb up to the ruin itself is steep – especially if you are hopelessly unfit like me.

Dundonald is the forgotten castle of Scottish history, certainly for my generation. What little I know of this country's past has been gleaned in my adult years. I was told little while I was at school, where history teachers were more interested in droning on about Corn Laws and Poor Laws. I have a vague recollection of being told about Bannockburn but that's about all.

Although nothing particularly dark occurred here at Dundonald (apart from it being destroyed by Robert the Bruce during an English occupation) it is the springboard for all sorts of events through history. For this is where the Stewart line began – the same Stewarts who became kings of Scotland and then of Britain, spawned a queen who managed to propel her country into civil war, caused the blood and thunder of the Covenanters' rebellion and produced pretenders to the throne who sparked the carnage of the various Jacobite rebellions.

It all began in 1124 when the Scottish King David I decided that the English system of government was better than that of his own country. The Scots were prone to fighting among themselves and really getting nowhere fast (perhaps nothing much has changed) and because he so admired the Norman way of life, Davey-boy decided to import some English families north to bring some order. One such knight was Walter Fitzallan, whose father had come to these shores on the Hastings package tour with William the Conqueror. Walter was an old buddy of David's from his days in England and was quickly made the King's Steward, basically to keep an eye on the royal loot. The King in turn gave his pal vast chunks of land in Ayrshire, Renfrewshire, Argyll, Bute and the Lothians.

Walter took a look at his lands and decided he fancied building a castle at Dundonald from where he set about the business of founding a dynasty, with each son and grandson becoming the High Steward. As the years passed, they became better known as the Stewards rather than the Fitzallans. It was a small step, then, to the name Stewart, which was later Frenchified to Stuart by Mary Queen of Scots.

From the start the Stewarts were neck-deep in Scottish politics. David's idea of the Normans bringing order to his troubled land never really worked – the Scottish nobles still bickered and fought, always keeping their country divided and the Stewarts were in there conniving with the best of them. It was this propensity for deception, betrayal and selfishness among Scottish nobles that Edward Plantagenet played on during the Wars of Independence.

One High Steward, also called Walter, first supported William Wallace against Edward, then changed sides and fought against the Scots at Stirling Bridge, only to turn his coat once again when he saw the tide of battle was going against the English. He fought alongside Bruce at Bannockburn, staying loyal this time, and was rewarded with the hand of the King's daughter Marjory in marriage.

Walter and Marjory had a son, named Robert Bruce Stewart, born prematurely after his mother suffered a fatal fall from a horse. The hasty delivery by Caesarean section left him slightly crippled for life. This Stewart began the royal line in 1371 when he was crowned King Robert II on the death of his uncle, the Bruce's son, David II. The royal line he spawned lasted 333 years. His son, Robert III (clearly, Scotland was never short of a Bob or two), came to power in 1390 and eventually moved his court to Edinburgh and Stirling. Although no

DEVIL'S GALLOP

longer the seat of power, Dundonald remained in Stewart hands for another 200 years.

For many years Dundonald lay neglected and untended, as so many historic sites are. But now Historic Scotland owns the site. They have built a visitors' centre and restored certain parts of the castle's interior. It may not be as glorious as it once was, but at least the visitor can get a feel for the history of the place.

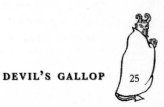

FOUR
Braveheart

I left Dundonald, travelling towards the A78. Following the signs for Ayr, I eventually come to the Monktonhall roundabout and then the village of Monkton which perches on the edge of Prestwick Airport's runway. I followed signs for British Aerospace and found, on the left near the entrance to that company's premises, a small kirkyard with a ruined church. This is the site of the last resting place of Ann Burns, great niece of the poet and daughter of the Rev. Thomas Burns, who was the minister here. But you'll have guessed that's not why I had come.

According to one of Blind Harry's more whimsical stories, Wallace was near here when he had a dream about a man presenting him with a magnificent sword on a mountain so high he could see the whole of Scotland. The land below was on fire and Wallace was told it was his destiny to right the wrongs that had been done to his country. In the dream, a beautiful woman gave Wallace a red and green wand and made the sign of the saltire on his face with a sapphire, giving him a cross look.

When Wallace awoke, he asked the priest of the old church what his dream meant and was told the man must have been St Andrew and the woman the Virgin Mary. The red part of the wand, Wallace was told, signified battles and the green courage.

The tale helps turn Wallace from a hot-tempered, patriotic warrior into a man with a mission; a hero whose destiny was sealed from birth. If he did have this dream, then it would have spurred him on to take his next step, turning the land around Ayr red with English blood.

I was now very much in Burns country and a glance at a tourist map shows just how many Burns sites there are in this area. Scotland's national bard had his share of dark moments. He was a hard drinker and those binges could often lead to violent rages (just ask his lassie Jean Armour). But he was also fiercely proud of his country and was a big fan of William Wallace. I left Monkton, and headed again for the A77. My next site links these two men.

Just before I came to the Whitletts roundabout, there was a sign for the small village of St Quivox. Pausing only to wonder how the hell a French hamlet came to be situated in deepest Ayrshire, I turned left at the roundabout and onto the B743. I then took a right and, once past the Scottish Agricultural College at Auchincruive, I crossed a stone bridge – Oswald's Bridge, named after a former landowner – and found on the right a gate leading to a small hummock (which is like a hillock but more musical). There is a cairn here, dedicated to both Wallace and Burns, and the wood surrounding it is what is left of Leglen Wood, where Wallace hid under the protection of a kinsman who owned Auchincruive after the unpleasantness over the fish at the River Irvine.

Robert Burns had read Blind Harry's Wallace epic and this great tale of patriotism, adventure and romance so filled his poet's heart that he said it would stay with him until the day he died. Or as he more picturesquely put it: 'The story of Wallace poured a Scottish prejudice into my veins which will boil along until the floodgates of life shut in eternal rest.' (But that's poets for you – never use one word where ten would do.) Burns would often walk in this wood, exploring 'every den and dell where I supposed my heroic countryman might have sheltered'. It was during these visits that his heart 'glowed with a wish to be able to make a song on him equal to his merits'. Although Burns never wrote anything about Wallace directly, he did come up with the lyric for *Scots Wha Hae*, said to be based on the words of Bruce at Bannockburn. Unfortunately, there is little left of the wood itself and after all these years it is difficult to believe that Wallace could hide here from a blind man with a hearing aid and blocked nose, let alone English troops.

On leaving the cairn, I retraced my route back to the A77 and made my way across the Whitletts roundabout and into Ayr town centre for the next part of my tour, which involves more of Wallace, a bit of Bruce and a touch of the supernatural.

FIVE

The Town of Honest Men

There has been a settlement at the mouth of the River Ayr since the Mesolithic age. It has grown considerably since then, of course, and by 1263 it was a port important enough to attract the interest of King Haakon of Norway, who – they say – planned to take the town as a prelude to dominating the rest of the Scottish mainland. However, a storm hit his fleet in the Firth of Clyde and his men were forced to take on the Scottish forces at Largs instead. (Either that or they heard you got a better ice cream cone at Nardini's.)

The English, though, were more successful. They invaded Ayr in 1296, taking over the castle and garrisoning the troops at the Barns of Ayr, which may have been at the south-eastern end of Mill Wynd behind Ayr High Street. When Wallace was a young man, 18 Scottish nobles were massacred in the Barns (this scene formed the opening of *Braveheart*) and after his Monkton vision, Wallace decided to put the Barns to flame. He had the roofs covered with pitch and had other pieces of wood piled at the sides to assist the bonfire. When the flames took hold, the English troops tried to escape through any exit they could find, but Wallace had stationed stout-hearted and well-armed men at each one who slaughtered the fleeing soldiers and tossed their bodies back into the inferno.

As the sky turned black with smoke and the screams of the men dying inside rent the air, Wallace rode out of Ayr. He stopped on a hill overlooking the town, between Craigie and Tarbolton, looked back at his handiwork and commented, 'The Barns of Ayr burn weil.' While some historians believe that Wallace did not slaughter the garrison, but merely destroyed the Barns to prevent them from being used again, according to legend, that was how Barnweill Hill got its name. A memorial tower can actually be seen from the A77 as you travel south from Kilmarnock. It stands between some thin trees on the crest of the low hills to the left.

Ayr castle stood close to where the swimming pool is now, although no trace of it remains. Robert the Bruce destroyed it in 1298 and then again in 1312 (clearly a man who believed that if you try something once, you should try, try again). The fortified walls near the harbour are the remains of the massive citadel built in 1654 by Cromwell's forces, who supposedly used stones taken from Ardrossan Castle. The turret sticking out of the wall facing the modern swimming baths is known as Miller's Folly, after the Ayr eccentric John 'Baron' Miller, who bought the land once covered by the citadel and added windows onto an old sentinel post.

To find the heart of the old citadel, I made my way beyond this wall to St John's Tower, which stands alone in a small patch of green in a quiet residential neighbourhood. Cromwell's troops used this as an armoury and it is all that remains of the medieval church of St John, although the tower itself was not added until the fourteenth century. It was here that Robert the Bruce attended a Scottish Parliament in 1315, after Bannockburn. John Knox came here to preach (his son-in-law was minister for six years from 1600), while his daughter Elizabeth is said to be buried somewhere beside the tower. Knox's hated Mary Queen of Scots stabled her horses here for a night in 1563 (although the inscription 'Mary Queen of Scots' horses slept here' wouldn't be much of a tourist attraction). The walk from here to the Citadel Walls gives one some idea of just how big the damn thing was. It is a shame nothing more remains of the structure.

Maggie Osborne is said to be buried in the yard of this tower. She was an innkeeper who had, if the charges against her are to be believed, enjoyed a neat sideline in witchcraft – so why she is buried on consecrated ground is a mystery. There are many stories about her, including how she used the black arts to sink a ship in Ayr harbour because some sailor had somehow upset her. She also turned herself into a beetle on one occasion to avoid confrontation with a minister. A shepherd almost crushed her with his cart and she was so incensed that she placed a curse on him. Not long after, the hapless man, his wife and ten children were all killed in a freak snowstorm.

That someone called Maggie Osborne existed there can be no

doubt, but her eventual execution for witchcraft cannot be substantiated. She may also have been confused with one Maggie Wallace, who was burned at the stake in 1629.

Executions have taken place in various parts of the town over the centuries. Ayr's gallows once stood a few hundred yards away from what is now the railway station before being moved to the common south of the town. In 1809 a new gallows was erected on the doorway of the tollbooth at New Bridge Street. This was demolished in 1825 and it is said that the two large rectangular stones with square central holes, still visible in the exterior wall of the Gartferry Hotel in Racecourse Road, were the very stones used to support the gibbet.

In 1821, a new prison and courthouse were built on the west side of Wellington Square, where the county buildings now stand. The prison, which inmates affectionately dubbed 'the cottage by the sea', had its own gallows at the southern corner of its western wall. In Glasgow, men were condemned to die 'facing the monument' on Glasgow Green. In Ayr the condemned met their maker 'facing Arran'; a much more picturesque exit – when you can see the isle through the mist and rain.

The first man to be executed here in 1822 was a rapist. The last was Girvan man Alexander Cunningham in 1854, who shot his wife Janet through a window with his fowling-piece. Naturally, he was convicted of fowl play. The prison was finally demolished in 1931.

Ayr, like other places in Scotland, is proud of its association with Wallace. There is a statue of him on the Wallace Tower. This building's links to Wallace, or any of the family, are unclear, although a plaque on the wall suggests it is on the site of a tollbooth in which Wallace was once imprisoned. There is another, smaller, sculpture on a building on the corner of Newmarket Street and High Street, known as the 'Wee Wallace'. From the ground, the statue looks as if Wallace had duck's disease (his bum being too near the ground), but this short look was necessary to fit the statue in the niche.

Wallace was well known in Ayr – and not just for his propensity for pyrotechnics, as displayed in the Barns of Ayr episode. While he was hiding in Leglen Woods, he would often come into the town seeking recreation. He was a young man and even though destined for greatness, he had a young man's urges – and Ayr was full of bonnie lasses, as Burns later noted.

DEVIL'S GALLOP

On one such visit, an Englishman was offering locals the chance to beat him on the back with a stick. He was charging them one groat (about four pennies) for the privilege and a few were taking up the challenge. After all, it wasn't every day an invader gave them the chance to vent their animosity. But the Englishman was a big lad so he took the blows easily and was soon getting everyone's groat. Wallace took up the challenge, parted with the lucre and promptly broke the man's spine.

But it was not this encounter that led to his incarceration in the tollbooth. It was on a later trip – when for the second time Wallace killed a man over fish. You'd think by then he'd have taken the hint and become a vegan.

Wallace was carrying a basketload of seafood through the town when an English steward demanded that he hand it over. Wallace, being Wallace, refused and the man came at him with a quarter-staff. As we know, Wallace was not the kind of chap to stand there and just take it, so he pulled his dagger and killed the steward on the spot. This time, though, there would be no hiding in Leglen Wood, for English troops surrounded him and carted him off to the tollbooth.

Conditions in these early prisons would give the Howard League for Penal Reform the vapours. Life was hard and Wallace eventually contracted dysentery and fell into a coma. The jailers, believing him dead, dragged him from the cell and threw him over a wall, where they expected him to rot. News of Wallace's death reached his old nurse who rolled up on a cart to claim the corpse. She realised that Wallace was not in fact dead, and instead of wrapping him in a winding sheet and planting him in the ground, she wrapped him in a blanket and plied him with the medieval version of chicken soup, Lucozade and colouring books.

Because Cromwell's troops had taken over the Church of St John the Baptist for their armoury, the Lord Protector agreed to stump up the necessaries to build a new church, to be situated behind the High Street, on the banks of the river. The kirkyard is reached from the bustling modern street by way of a cobbled lane and through an old lychgate adorned by two examples of old mortsafes; heavy metal girdles which were placed over coffins to stop bodysnatchers from indulging in a spot of resurrectionism.

It is here in this quiet place that we find a particularly interesting Covenanter memorial. Seven of the rebels were buried here after being executed in the town as a warning to others not to follow in their path. Eight men had been due to face the noose originally – and thereby hangs a tale, if not the eighth Covenanter.

The men had been captured at Rullion Green in the Pentland Hills (see Border Raid). Twelve men in total were tried in Ayr, found guilty and sentenced to death; the hangings to be split between Ayr, Irvine in the north and Dumfries in the south. The bulk of the condemned – eight of them – were to die in Ayr, but the public hangman found he had pressing business elsewhere. The hangman from Irvine, a Covenanter sympathiser who did not balk at executing witches, was summoned but he also refused. He was thrown into the tollbooth and guarded while local worthies unsuccessfully tried to force, cajole or frighten him into plying his trade.

It was then the judges hit on a novel idea – they would offer one of the eight men his life in return for turning executioner. After some time, Ayr man Cornelius Anderson agreed and on 27 December 1666 he despatched his erstwhile friends on the gibbet fixed to the tollbooth wall. It is said he was so drunk on brandy that he really did not know what he was doing. A few days later, Anderson's new skills were pressed into service once again, this time to hang the two men in Irvine. They are both buried in Irvine's kirkyard.

Anderson found himself treated as a pariah throughout the country and later fled to Ireland, a broken man, where he died in a fire.

It is a sad little tale from a period filled with sad little tales and Auld Kirk of Ayr was a fitting place to end my short visit to the town.

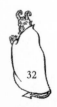

DEVIL'S GALLOP

SIX

Feudin', Fussin' and Fightin'

I left the town, not by the A77 for a change, but by the pretty way – the A719 coast road, following signs for Maidens.

On the outskirts of Ayr, looking over a wall opposite the old racecourse, I glimpsed the ruins of Greenan Castle on its rocky heights above the shore. Anyone who wants to get to the castle should follow the signs for Doonfoot where they can park in a small car park, then walk along the beach to the rocky cliff on which the ruined castle stands. The land beneath the castle is slowly being eroded and I suppose it's only a matter of time before it tumbles onto the beach below. So I'd keep looking up if I were you.

In 1602 Sir Thomas Kennedy set out from here to ride to Edinburgh. In the woods of St Leonard's near Ayr, he was ambushed and murdered by followers of the Kennedies of Bargany, his kinsfolk. To understand why family members would turn on each other I must turn to another castle, one with a much darker history than Greenan's.

A few miles further down the coast, the village of Dunure and its ruined castle sits on the edge of the water. Leaving the A719 I drove downhill through some pretty impressive – and expensive – real estate until I reached the old harbour. From a pebble-covered cove I enjoyed a dramatic view of the castle, standing dark against the sun. I sat a while here, watching a swan drift lazily on the smooth water, listening to the waves whispering on the shingle, and considered a tale of a noble family divided by hatred – a tale of murder, betrayal and ultimate retribution.

For centuries the Kennedies were such a force to be reckoned with in this area that they were dubbed 'the Kings of Carrick'. The family name is derived from Kenneth, which in Gaelic signifies 'chief', and as such is common among Pictish and Scottish lords. Variations of this are Kened, Cinaed, Cinaeda, and Kenedus. This leads to MacKenede ('son of Kenneth') and in 1185 a Henry MacKenede appears as one of the rebel leaders fighting against Roland, Lord of Galloway, who fell in battle on 5 July 1185.

Another forefather of the Kennedies (a MacKenane) was the man who first came into possession of Dunure Castle, at least according to legend. In October 1262, he had been part of Alexander III's army defending Scottish soil against Haakon's Norse invaders at Largs and had followed a force of retreating Vikings down the coast. The Norsemen holed up in a castle on a crag – possibly Dunure – and settled in for a siege. The MacKenane gang launched a successful attack and managed to kill every last Dane in the place, for which a grateful King Alexander granted the MacKenanes the lands of Carrick.

And so began the great Kennedy dynasty of Carrick, sparking someone to dash off the immortal lines:

> The Kennedies wi' a their power
> frae Cassillis to Ardstinchar Tower.

It was John Kennedy of Dunure who first brought the lands of Cassillis, around Maybole, into the Kennedy fold (perhaps by marrying Marjorie Montgomery, whose family owned them). But the family's love of a bit of bloodshed would stay with them through the centuries – and if they could not fight the enemies outside the family, they would find some within. In 1408, John Kennedy's grandson was killed in a quarrel with his half-brother Gilbert, thus setting the tone for over two centuries of family squabbles that often ended at the point of a sword.

It was at Dunure that John Mor MacDonald was killed when talks between his independently-minded clan and James I's representative James Campbell broke down in 1429, prompting a rebellion that ended with the King's army being defeated at Inverlochy Castle. Dunure was used, no doubt, because the Kennedies were neutral observers in the affair. Meanwhile, Hugh and Gilbert Kennedy sided with Joan of Arc when she ended the siege of Orleans – also in 1429.

At the disastrous Battle of Solway Moss in November 1542, the

DEVIL'S GALLOP

Third Earl of Cassillis (another Gilbert) was taken hostage and held prisoner in England. Here he met Archbishop of Canterbury Thomas Cranmer, an ardent follower of Henry's Church of England. Cranmer managed to talk Gilbert into renouncing the Pope's authority and in 1453 the Scotsman was set free in return for £1000 ransom from his family and his promise that he would support Henry's claims to be overlord of Scotland. Mary had succeeded to the throne on the death of her father shortly after Solway Moss, and Kennedy also agreed to help deliver her into the hands of her Uncle Henry, who thought a marriage to his young son was just the thing to bring him the Scottish crown. Henry never did get his fleshy fingers on the child, or the crown for that matter. (Mary Queen of Scots, incidentally, later slept at Dunure Castle, during a royal tour of the West Coast.)

Meanwhile, Gilbert offered to organise the assassination of Cardinal Beaton – a stalwart supporter of the new Queen and her mother, Mary of Guise. 'The King did not mislike the offer' reads a contemporary report, which is not surprising as Henry was never one to balk at anyone's death, especially a religious leader's. Although Gilbert went off the notion, Beaton was murdered in 1546, much to the joy of John Knox (see Rebel March). Henry himself did not long outlive the fat, cruel Cardinal, dying in January 1547.

That same year, following the siege of St Andrews (see Rebel March), a register surfaced bearing the names of Scots nobles who had sworn allegiance to England and naturally Cassillis was one of them. However, the canny Gilbert had already declared his loyalty to the Regent, the Earl of Arran, his patriotism couched in defiant terms. Rather than be subject to England, Gilbert said, Scots would 'dye, every mother's sonne of us'. In 1557, this now loyal subject of the young Queen formed part of a commission sent to France to negotiate her marriage to the Dauphin. The deal was struck at the Louvre but on the return journey, Gilbert and other members of his party met a mysterious end at Dieppe. It was said they were poisoned by the French for refusing to give France sovereignty over Scotland as part of the dowry. On the other hand, John Knox and followers were in Dieppe at around this time. Could it be they had a hand in punishing those who were selling Scottish Protestantism down the river? Oliver Stone could make a movie out of this.

DEVIL'S GALLOP

But it is the third Earl's son, also called Gilbert, who brings us back again to the castle of Dunure. Like his dad, he continued to support Queen Mary, fighting for her at Langside, but smartly transferring his loyalties to her son, James VI, while Mary languished in various English castles, awaiting Queen Betty's royal whim. This particular Gilbert was the first of his line to become known as the King of Carrick, thanks to his rapacious empire building through south-west Scotland. He is said to have used a monk to forge a document ceding the lands held by Glenluce Abbey to him. Not only did he have the monk murdered to cover his tracks but he also had his hired killer fitted up for theft and hanged. Clearly, the activities of the fourth Earl of Carrick would make the Borgias drop their poisons in shock. But it was a notorious barbecue to which he invited the abbot of Crossraguel that earns him a place in dark legend.

Gilbert's uncle Quintin had been abbot until his death in 1564, when the Earl took possession of the buildings. The abbey was quite a prize, for although the number of monks who lived there had declined during the Reformation (by 1564 there was only one) it still commanded substantial rents, teinds and duties. However one year after abbot Quintin's death, the King appointed Alan Stewart as lay commendator, and he took back the lands – and their rents. Gilbert took exception to this and a game of fiscal cat and mouse developed between the two wily men. The fiery Earl's anger increased when Stewart developed an alliance with Thomas Kennedy of Bargany, who held lands around Ballantrae and Girvan, and who fiercely disputed Cassillis's claims to be the dominant force of the Kennedy clan. Finally, Gilbert decided he'd had enough of these shenanigans and in August 1570 he had the commendator kidnapped as he walked in woods near to the abbey.

Stewart was thrown into the dark vault at Dunure, of which nothing now remains (if it ever existed) where Gilbert, according to the commendator's later complaint to the Privy Council 'denudit me of all my cleathis, perforce, except onlie my sark and doublet'. They then tied him in his sark and doublet to a spit and stoked the fire, roasting the man like a pig, thrusting an apple into his mouth to stifle his screams. The idea was to force Stewart to sign over the deeds to the abbey lands. After hours of this torture, the man duly did as he

DEVIL'S GALLOP

was told. He remained imprisoned in the dark vault for a further three months, until Kennedy of Bargany stormed up to Dunure Castle with a hefty force of outraged men.

'Give us the abbot,' they cried.

'Shan't!' came the reply from the battlements, along with a medieval gesture or two. However Bargany's men were not to be denied and eventually stormed the castle to free the severely singed prisoner. As soon as he was safe, the commendator naturally reneged on the deal and reported Gilbert to the Privy Council, which delivered a sharp blow to the errant Earl's wrist, fining him £2,000 and telling him not to do it again.

Gilbert did finally take possession of much of the abbey's lands, but through purchase rather than extortion. He died in 1576 when his horse fell on him. Alan Stewart lived until 1587, still showing off the scars of his time in the torture chamber. But the foul deeds in the dark vault would live on in legend, amid claims that on dark nights when the wind is soft from the sea, you can still hear the screams of the roasting abbot from deep within the bowels of the castle ruins.

Moving on from Dunure, I passed by the curious phenomenon that is the Electric Brae (by a trick of topography you appear to be travelling uphill when in fact you are going down). Looking down the coast on the right, I saw another castle – in somewhat better repair than Dunure. This is Culzean Castle, another stronghold of the Kennedies. However, the present structure bears little relation to the early fortification, having been extensively re-modelled in the eighteenth century by architect Robert Adam for the Marquis of Ailsa. The picturesque grounds are worth a wander, and there are plenty of places for a quick – if somewhat pricey – bite to eat, while the castle interior is interesting. In 1945, the National Trust for Scotland gave General (later President) Dwight D. Eisenhower the top floor of the castle in recognition of his service as Supreme Commander of Allied Forces during the Second World War. Eisenhower visited the castle many times during his lifetime, but only once while he was President. It is said he held a great affection for Scotland.

A phantom piper is said to play at this castle, and there is a tale told of a little boy who asked the Laird o' Co' (apparently the Lords of Culzean were so called because of the number of coves near to the castle) if he could fill his panniken with some beer for his sick mum, presumably to wash an aspirin down. The Laird very kindly said yes and the little lad took over half a barrel's worth before his panniken was filled. That must have been some panniken – not to mention one hell of an aspirin. Years later, the Laird was imprisoned in some foreign hellhole after being captured in battle and the door was thrown open to reveal the little boy who said: 'Laird o' Co', rise and go.' Outside the prison, the boy told the Laird to get up on his back and almost immediately afterwards he was back at his castle at Culzean. 'Ane guid turn deserves anither,' rhymed the lad, 'tak ye that for being sae kin' to my auld mither . . .' The boy was one of the fairy folk, who obviously rhymed for no reason, and I'll bet the Kennedy involved in this tale was glad he had put on his charitable hat the day they first met.

Around 1579, Sir Thomas Kennedy of Culzean became the tutor of his brother Gilbert's son John, the fifth Earl of Cassillis, who was only eight years old when his dad found out that horse riding can be bad for your health. Sir Tom was an ambitious man and not above a little direct action when he felt like it (he was in fact one of Alan Stewart's kidnappers). In 1579 he carried off Elizabeth McGill from her father's home and made her his wife. She had previously been married to Robert Logan of Restalrig, who found himself in deep water after being implicated in the Gowrie Conspiracy against James VI (see Rebel March). However, when Kennedy was taken to court for the abduction, the lady testified that she had gone willingly.

Kennedy had his own ambitions to be Earl but drew the line at murdering the youngster. The next best thing was to wield power as the lad's tutor but that was snatched from his grasp when the King appointed Lord Glamis as young John's guardian. However, Sir Thomas finally had his stab at the position when Glamis was killed in a street brawl in 1579 in Stirling. History does not record whether Kennedy had anything to do with this, although he was involved in a plot to assassinate his kinsman, Gilbert Kennedy of Bargany, some years later. To learn more of this, I left Culzean and turned left, back the way I came until I once again reached the junction leading back to Dunure. Carrying on straight ahead, I was soon deep in the heart of Maybole.

Maybole is the ancient capital of Carrick and, if the width of the main street is anything to go by, has not changed much over the centuries. If ever there was a town that needed a bypass it is Maybole. The A77 runs right through the heart of it, complete with convoys of lorries making their way to and from Stranraer. All it takes is for two or three people to park their cars in the narrow street and it becomes bottleneck alley.

There is a castle at the junction of Cassillis Street (formerly the stockyards for the Earls) and High Street. This privately owned building was the town house of the Kings of Carrick and was probably an imposing building in its day, but someone with a severe dose of roughcast fever struck at some time in the past and ruined the look of it. It was here on 11 December 1601 that John, the fifth Earl, now grown into manhood, heard that his arch enemy, Gilbert, Laird of Bargany, was going to pass close by on his way from Ayr to his home near Girvan. According to John's later defence, he learned that Bargany had with him a number of men for whom there were arrest warrants outstanding. As the local bigwig, he claimed he had authorisation to pursue with fire and sword outlaws such as Hew Kennedy of Bennan and Thomas Kennedy of Drumurchy – both of whom were related to him. For the Kennedies, blood was somewhat thinner than H$_2$O.

And so Cassillis, with the approval of his old tutor Sir Thomas Kennedy of Culzean, rode out from Maybole Castle with some 200 men to confront the much smaller Bargany force at Pennyglen. As a result of the subsequent clash, Gilbert of Bargany, despite gallant resistance, was 'schamefullie, cruellie and unmercifullie' slain. He was carried off to Ayr but died within a matter of hours, at the age of 25. The Earl escaped punishment, claiming to the investigating Privy Council that as Earl, and with the power of the pit and gallows, he had every right to attempt to apprehend the outlaws. So if they resisted, then he was perfectly correct in using force.

Young Bargany's death so outraged his followers, including John Mure of Auchendrane (his was an estate which lies between Maybole and Minishant on the road back to Ayr) that they plotted revenge. They could not strike directly at Cassillis, for he was too well guarded and his death would provoke strong action from the King. However, they could exact justice from the Earl's advisor, Sir Thomas Kennedy of Culzean. And so steps were taken that would lead to what Sir Walter Scott would later call 'Auchendrane, or the Ayrshire Tragedy'.

On 12 May 1602, Sir Thomas called in at the home of his kinsman John Kennedy, at Greenan Castle, on his way to Edinburgh. He was later murdered at Duppil Burn, in St Leonard's, now part of Ayr. For a number of years, the identity of his assassins remained a secret, but according to legend they were eventually brought to justice through a bizarre incident involving an innocent young relative of theirs and a murdered soldier. But that particular tale must wait for now.

Maybole is not the prettiest of towns in Scotland, or even Ayrshire for that matter, but it is steeped in history. The town acted as the focal point for all sorts of goings-on between the warring Kennedies, who regularly faced each other down in the narrow streets like some Hibernian Montagues and Capulets. Swords were drawn, hackbutts were aimed and blood spilled on many occasions here.

However, the Kennedies did more for the town than kill people. They also built the Auld Collegiate Church in 1371. Lying behind Main Street, the church – now a ruin – is the final resting place for many of the old clan including: David, the first Earl who fell at Flodden in 1513; Gilbert, the second Earl, who was murdered in Prestwick; Gilbert, the third Earl, poisoned at Dieppe; Gilbert, the fourth Earl, who made the commendator of Crossraguel feel so toasty; and John, known as 'the grave and solemn Earl', who was a staunch defender of the Scottish church. But more on him later.

Gilbert, the abbot's torturer, was said to be in league with the Devil, using a black raven as a familiar. The demonic bird was present during the three-month barbecue in Dunure, whispering encouragement in the Earl's ear as the spit turned. On the night Gilbert died, the captain of a ship passing near to Ailsa Craig (that lump of volcanic rock sticking out of the waters a few miles seaward of Culzean) claimed to have seen a very strange sight indeed. He saw a fiery chariot being pulled by horses of flame across the surface of the water. The brave captain hailed the driver and asked where he was headed.

'From Hell to Cassillis,' boomed a voice, 'for the soul of the Earl!'
Later the captain saw the chariot making its return journey.

Writhing in the back, and howling against the fierce winds, was the Earl.

When the coffin was being transported from Dunure to the Collegiate Church, a large black crow landed on the funeral bier. The horses refused to move until the crow had flown off.

These tales, it is worth noting, were also told about Gilbert's descendant Sir Archibald Kennedy who was a ferocious persecutor of the Covenanters. When he died in 1710, it was rumoured he had also been carried off by the Devil.

The kirk was last used as a place of worship in April 1563. By that time, reformation zeal was sweeping Scotland and celebrating mass was declared illegal. John Knox – that fiery advocate of the new religion – had already visited the town in 1562 and taken part in a debate with the abbot of Crossraguel, Quintin Kennedy, over the nature of the mass. The argument raged in the provost's house and, with neither side gaining an advantage, it ended in a draw. A plaque on the side of a modern house in what is now called 'John Knox's Vennel' marks the site of the old house.

However the auld kirk still had something to add to local history. An Act of Parliament may have made mass illegal but a band of 200 local Roman Catholics were not going to take it lying down. Soon after the Act was passed, they gathered in the chapel determined to worship their God in their own way – and they had with them a number of 'speris, gunnis and other wappins' to make their point forcibly if necessary. The congregation said their mass and their leaders were promptly arrested and fined.

For my final Kennedy tale, I shall return to the castle. Above a door facing the street is a series of carved heads. It is said these are not gargoyles, as you might expect, but the likenesses of gypsies who had been hanged by the grave and solemn sixth Earl. His hatred for travelling people is said to stem from the fact that his wife ran off with Jack Faa, who was either of Romany stock or a dark-skinned, curly-haired noble from Dunbar, depending on which account you read.

Anyway, before Lady Jean married the Earl, she had met Jack and fallen in love with him. But her father was determined she would marry well and the powerful King of Carrick was the man for him. So Jean was wed and packed off to Cassillis to stay. Jack, however, was not one to let such a passion as theirs die, so he followed her with his gypsy band, managing to sneak into Cassillis while the Earl was away at the Westminster Assembly in 1643. He and Jean ran off together, but Kennedy, returned from the south, pursued them and hanged the would-be Romeo and his band from the nearest tree. Taking his errant bride back to Maybole, he imprisoned her in a high room in the castle. There she remained for the rest of her days, staring out of the window at the busy High Street or working on a tapestry that told the story of her life and tragic love. The tapestry has since disappeared but you can still see the oriel (projecting) window on the top floor from which she stared wistfully at life passing below and thought of her dead gypsy lover.

This is a touching little tale but it's unlikely to be true. The sixth Earl did attend the Westminster Assembly of 1643 – but his wife had already been a dead a year. And letters still exist showing that during their 21 years of marriage he continued to hold great affection for her. But these are mere facts. I prefer the romantic version.

SEVEN

A King is Born

I left Maybole via the A77, passing Baltersan Castle – a ruined keep that an enterprising businessman hopes to renovate and turn into an up-market hotel. Soon after, I saw the ruins of Crossraguel Abbey, which is well worth a visit.

Kirkoswald was home, a sign told me, of Souter Johnnie, one of the characters featured in Burns's poem *Tam O'Shanter*. His thatched cottage (or rather that of cobbler John Davidson on whom Souter Johnnie was based) is now a museum but as he did nothing remotely dark – except a spot of soutering here and there – it held no interest for me. My attentions were focused on the churchyard and its ruined kirk at the southern end of the village. This is quite an ancient burial ground, the plaque on the gates told me, now internationally renowned for the graves not only of Johnnie, but also of the real-life inspirations for the innkeeper's wife Kirkton Jean, and Tam O'Shanter (Douglas Graham) himself. Burns's grandparents are buried here, while the poet himself attended school in the village.

According to legend, St Oswald fought a battle here in 634 AD and built the first church as a way of saying 'thanks' to God for being on his side. This later became a shrine until the monks from Crossraguel built a more permanent church in 1244. Quintin Kennedy and John Knox, around the time of their great debate in nearby Maybole, preached against each other's ideas here in 1562.

There is another gravestone of interest. It is that of a gamekeeper who was shot by a poacher and like many markers from the period, it tells a most fascinating story. The stone was raised by the Marquis of Ailsa, the descendant of the Kennedies, and commemorates:

Richard Jones, one of his assistant gamekeepers who while in the discharge of his duty was shot dead by Thomas Ross, a noted Maybole poacher, in Park Glen on the sabbath 16-1-1859. Jones was a faithful servant and a steady well-doing man. He died in the 29th year of his age and left a widow and two young children to mourn his untimely end. Ross was tried for the cowardly crime and having pled guilty of culpable homicide was sentenced to penal servitude for life.

The gamekeeper's wife Margaret is also buried in the graveyard, having died on 19 December 1862 at the age of 34.

Inside the ruined church lies an ancient font, roughly hewn out of local stone. It was here, they say, that one of Scotland's greatest heroes was christened. Later, this canny political player and ferocious warrior would unite his country in a way that no one else ever could, and send the hated English scuttling back south after a blistering defeat at Bannockburn. And I had only to travel a few more short miles to see where he may have been born.

Turnberry sits at the junction of the A77 and the A719 coast road. I could have been here sooner had I not diverted to Maybole, but then I would have missed all those wonderful Kennedy stories.

The village clusters at the foot of the imposing red-roofed Turnberry Hotel and looks out across its famed golf courses towards Ailsa Craig. I drove on past the houses and the hotel until I reached a point where the road widened enough on either side to park. From here I was just a walk away from finding what little is left of Robert the Bruce's birthplace. A short distance in the Maidens direction I found a pathway to the left leading to the lighthouse. This lengthy stroll cut across the golf courses so I was careful not to deviate from the path, as this is private land and these people pay good money – and lots of it – for the privilege of battering a small white ball across the green. The wind and rain were attacking me horizontally from the sea but still there were men out playing golf. They're a different breed, I tell you.

As I walked against the wind like a mime act, I considered a bit more history. Before the Kennedies were lords of all they surveyed in Carrick, the real power lay with the Bruce clan. Of Norman stock, they had first come to this small island with William the Conqueror

DEVIL'S GALLOP

and thence to Scotland when King David thought it would be jolly good fun to import some English/Norman blood to Scotland. He gave lands in Annandale to the Bruce family (their name came from Brix, the town near Cherbourg from which they sprang) who took possession of Carrick in 1174 when Robert Bruce, the future king's father, married the Countess of Carrick. Their son Robert was born on 11 July 1274 – some say at Lochmaben Castle in Dumfriesshire, which was a Bruce seat. However, the strong favourite as his birthplace is here at Turnberry. There is little left of the castle, the ruins of which lie near to the lighthouse, battered by centuries of Scottish weather. The sea boils around the rocky shore, gusts of wind lifting spray and flinging it at the land. After being sandblasted for only half an hour, I felt somewhat eroded so just think of the effect hundreds of years of that kind of treatment has had on the ancient stone.

In 1286, the sudden death of King Alexander III plunged the country into turmoil. His daughter, the seven-year-old Margaret, Maid of Norway, was to be the new ruler, which did not please the nobles overmuch. They were far from delighted at the prospect of being ruled by an infant, and by extension a series of power-hungry regents. And so a deputation was sent south to the child's great-uncle, Edward Plantagenet, King of England. And what a mistake *that* turned out to be. Edward already saw himself as Lord Paramount of Scotland, thanks to an ill-advised oath of fealty on Alexander's part. Originally, the oath only related to the Scottish King's English lands but Edward took it to include everything north of Hadrian's Wall. Now, the confused Scots were coming to him to ask what to do about the inheritance problem, which really made him think he was cock-of-the-walk.

Edward decided it would be advisable for little Margaret to marry his son. That way, the crowns would be united under one strong ruler – and that ruler was Edward Longshanks (he was so called because he stood well over six feet in his stocking chain mail). Looking back, the idea made sense – so much sense that Henry VIII tried something similar three centuries later. Edward's reasoning was that Scotland would descend into anarchy without a steady hand on the throne, as the nobles would fight among themselves. And he wasn't far wrong.

Meanwhile, six 'guardians' of Scotland were appointed to govern

DEVIL'S GALLOP

the land. One was James, the High Steward. Another was Alexander Comyn, Earl of Buchan. The Bruce clan was left out in the cold – and this angered them immensely. They believed theirs was the stronger claim and the fact that the hated Comyns had gained such a foothold on the ladder to the top made them spit blood. It wasn't long before they were actually spilling it.

Edward's marriage plans for the youngsters never came to fruition, for Margaret died in Orkney, possibly of a severe bout of sea-sickness developed during the stormy crossing from her grandfather's court in Norway. This threw matters into deeper turmoil and the country was on the brink of civil war as 13 contenders for the throne came out of the woodwork. The two hot favourites, though, were Robert the Bruce, known as 'the competitor' and grandfather of the future king – and John Balliol, Lord of Galloway. Once again, Edward was asked to intercede and decide which claim carried more weight. Longshanks first obtained a promise from each claimant that they would recognise him as Lord Paramount of Scotland, then announced that Balliol should be King of Scots. The Bruces retired to their various strongholds to curse and scream at the wind in frustration.

Edward regarded Balliol as a puppet and demanded that he raise an army to fight in English wars against France. Balliol, though, showed a bit of backbone and refused, promptly forging a treaty with France that each country would come to the other's aid in time of trouble – the so-called Auld Alliance. Edward was incandescent with rage and, in 1296, set out to bring the troublesome Scots to heel once and for all. Robert the Bruce was by now 22 years of age and was already Earl of Carrick – his father resigned the title to him in 1292 to avoid swearing allegiance to Balliol. Now, with his grandfather dead a year and his father ready to side with Edward against the hated Balliol and Comyn clans, young Robert was about to be thrust centre stage in his country's struggle for independence . . .

But more of that later.

I left the windswept land that once was home to one of the country's greatest heroes and headed back across the golf course to the car. Driving back through Turnberry I rejoined the A77, following the sign for Girvan.

DEVIL'S GALLOP

EIGHT
Blood Test

From here the A77 follows the coastline and on a fine day is an enjoyable run, with long views of the deep, blue water stretching across the skyline until the profile of the jagged isle of Arran slices into the sky. Ailsa Craig – known as Paddy's Milestone because it is roughly halfway between Glasgow and Belfast – takes on what one guidebook calls 'a plum pudding shape' from here. It is the remnant plug of an ancient volcano and has been quarried for decades to make top-quality curling stones. They say a giant threw it at Scotland but his aim fell short. (A Glaswegian returned the compliment by chucking a beer can back at him.) There is a small castle on the island, which a band of Roman Catholics held for a short time during the Reformation, in the name of Spain. They were, however, soon forced to flee.

Beyond this craig can be seen the slim finger of the Kintyre Peninsula stretching out towards Ireland. If you are lucky and the air is clear and crisp, you will see the Emerald Isle itself on the horizon.

Smugglers used the many tiny inlets along this coastline to land their booty, always keeping a watchful eye for the revenue men. This practice was common all the way down the west coast of Ayrshire and Galloway to the Solway Firth.

As I approached Girvan, with the local football team's ground on the left, I spotted a small white marker-stone against the wall on the right. This marks the spot where Special Constable Alexander Ross was shot and killed on 12 July 1831, during an Orange Walk which turned into a riot.

The political climate that year did not bode well for such a march. The second reading of the Reform Bill had created no small measure of unrest, as it attempted to 'extend the right to vote to persons of property and intelligence'. An earlier Emancipation Bill had given Roman Catholics the right to stand for Parliament; now voters' rights were to be extended even further. Catholics were all for the Act, Protestants were none too happy – and as the anniversary of the Battle of the Boyne approached, passions ran high.

Girvan at that time had a population of around 6,000 and two-thirds of them were of Irish Catholic stock. That made the decision of the local lodge to invite a march by members from Crosshill, Dailly and Maybole Orange Lodges (the last being the first such lodge in the country, formed in 1799) all the more irritating. The feelings of the day were very much like the anger felt by both sides in modern-day Drumcree, where Ulster Protestants insist on marching through a staunchly Republican area. Nowadays, the army can be called in to keep the peace, but in 1831 Scotland it was a small force of special constables, many sworn in for the day, who were called upon by local magistrates. It was their job to see that the Orangemen took a route by-passing the town.

The two opposing forces met at roughly the spot where the marker-stone now sits. There were two or three hundred Orangemen, many armed with firearms and swords, faced by about 100 constables with only batons or sticks. In addition, about 400 women and children had gathered from the town to throw a few barbed comments – and eventually stones – at the marchers. At first, the leaders agreed to divert but their followers were not so amenable. They saw no reason why they could not march through the town, while the fusillade of rocks from the onlookers only exacerbated the situation.

It was during this confusion that Constable Alexander Ross was shot in the back. All hell broke loose and the Orangemen began to shoot, hack and slash at anyone who got in their way. The women and children fled across the fields to the safety of the river while some of the constables tried to restore order, but as they were outnumbered two or three to one, the task proved impossible. Before the officers could say 'Hello, hello, hello – what's going on here then' the Orangemen rolled over them like a huge wave, spilling into the town and flooding through the streets. One constable, Gilbert Davidson, was badly beaten and left for dead, while three of his colleagues were also sorely wounded; one losing the sight of an eye as a result, another

DEVIL'S GALLOP

being shot in the face. A policeman's lot that day was far from a happy one.

In all, 31 Maybole men were arrested and imprisoned at Ayr to await trial. The man who shot Constable Ross, Samuel Waugh, went on the run but was apprehended at Newton Stewart. He and march leader John Ramsay were both named on the murder indictment. They were subsequently tried in Edinburgh, because feelings were too high in their native Ayrshire, although only Waugh was found guilty. He died at a cottage by the sea, facing Arran. About 5,000 people turned out to watch him dangle before his body was sent back to Edinburgh for use by anatomists.

Girvan was a stronghold of the Kennedies of Bargany (the remains of the house of Bargany are situated to the east, on the road to Dailly) and in later years became a popular holiday resort. But like many of the resorts in Ayrshire it has declined in popularity, although it is still a favourite for day-trips and is a regular stopping point on the way to the ferry port of Stranraer. It also has a number of festivals throughout the year to attract visitors, including a popular folk festival.

The mystery of Sir Thomas Kennedy's murder was solved here. As you will remember, he was murdered as he rode from Greenan Castle towards Ayr on his way to Edinburgh. The only witness who was likely to have talked to the authorities about the murder was one William Dalrymple, who had carried word to the Mures of Auchendrane that Sir Thomas would be riding alone that day. But Dalrymple had disappeared soon after and there was no evidence to link the Mures with the ambush. Five years later, a body washed up on the shore between Girvan and Turnberry. Local farmer James Bannatyne identified it as being his nephew, William Dalrymple.

Dalrymple's body was laid out in a church in Girvan where Lady Kennedy of Culzean came to view it with a young girl in tow. As the youngster came closer, blood gushed from a wound on the back of the corpse's head. The child, it turned out, was the daughter of James Mure of Auchendrane – and this phenomenon pointed the finger at Dalrymple's murderer. Under the 'Ordeal by Blood theory', it was believed that if a murderer, or in this case the child of a murderer, came into close proximity with the victim's corpse, wounds would open and bleed. Within days, both Mure and his father John were arrested and thrown into Ayr tollbooth while further investigations were made. They were later taken to the infamous Heart of Midlothian gaol. For good measure, James Bannatyne was also apprehended and questioned. Neither of the Mures confessed but Bannatyne was not made of such stern stuff. He broke down and confessed at the first hint of torture, telling his questioners what had happened.

According to the farmer, young Will Dalrymple had carried a letter from Sir Thomas to his son-in-law James Mure, informing him of his impending trip to Edinburgh. Mure may have married Kennedy's daughter but he had no filial affection for the man so Kennedy was duly ambushed and Dalrymple disappeared, first being held in Auchendrane House and then at the home of a Mure family friend in Arran. But that was still too close for comfort for the murderers, so they had the youth packed off to war in Holland, in the hope that he would be slaughtered on some foreign field.

However Dalrymple confounded them all. He survived and returned five years later to his native Ayrshire soil, staying with his uncle James Bannatyne. The Mures panicked when they heard that the one man who could hang them had returned and arranged with Bannatyne to have Dalrymple meet them on the beach between Girvan and Turnberry. Bannatyne claimed he had no idea they meant to murder his kinsman – he thought they planned merely to kidnap him and have him sent away once more. But murder Dalrymple they did, the younger Mure beating and strangling him. The body was buried on the beach but was uncovered by the tide so it had to be dumped at sea. Dalrymple, though, proved to be just as much trouble in death as he was in life and the body floated back to shore, where it was found.

In Edinburgh, James Mure had his legs crushed in order to extract a confession. Although he steadfastly refused to talk, he and his father met their deaths on the Maiden, still proclaiming their innocence and accusing Bannatyne of perjury.

So ended the great Cassillis–Bargany feud. The Earl of Cassillis had emerged victorious and had assumed total control of the family, from Maybole to Galloway. Surprisingly, though, there is no lasting memorial to the feud; no Kennedy museum either in Maybole or Girvan. And that's a shame.

NINE

Seven Brides for Seven Dowries

The road between Girvan and Lendalfoot becomes increasingly dangerous, so a close watch has to be kept on the old speedometer – you never know when the way ahead will take a sudden turn or dip. It is, however, one of the most beautiful runs in Ayrshire, with rugged rocks rising out of sandy coves on the right and high cliffs towering above on the left. I've always thought it cried out for a helicopter shot in a movie.

Shortly after leaving Girvan I passed Ardmillan Castle Caravan Park. There is little left of the actual castle but Mary Queen of Scots slept here on one of her tours to rally support for her reign.

Finally, the various twists and turns levelled out (to an extent) and I caught sight of the tiny hamlet of Lendalfoot in the distance, made up mostly of wooden holiday homes set back from the road. It is said that there are tunnels linking Ardmillan Castle with smugglers' caves near here. Smugglers certainly did use these coves to land their goods before taking them on to the markets in Glasgow and Edinburgh.

The name Lendalfoot apparently harks back to when they spoke a form of Gaelic here and means 'At the mouth of the burn at the knoll of the fire signal', which would be very unwieldy on an Ordnance Survey map. This 'knoll of the fire signal' may well be a small rise to the east of the village, which is also known as Lousey Knowe. It seems that years ago, women took their children to the hill to search their heads for lice.

There is what appears to be an enclosed gravestone on the seaward side of the road. This was erected in memory of Archibald Hamilton and his crew who were drowned near this spot when their vessel sank on 11 September 1711. The mariners were from Arran, which can be seen (on a clear day) to the north-west. The message on the stone reads:

Ye passengers who ere ye are
As pass on this way
Disturb ye not this small respect
That's made to sailor's clay.

It is a sad reminder that, beautiful though the sea around here is, it can also be lethal.

On the hillside above the village stand the gaunt remains of Carlton Castle, now part of a farmyard. This was the home of the Cathcart family, who as the 'De Kathkerkes' came to Scotland with David I's Norman immigrants. Sir William De Kathkerke swore fealty to Edward I after the sack of Berwick before choosing to support the Scots in their struggle for independence. He was taken captive, thought it politic to change his mind again, and subsequently fought on the English side. His son, Sir Alane, suffered from no such confusion. He pledged allegiance to Robert the Bruce and followed Bruce's brother Edward on his raid into Galloway in the summer of 1308. During the Cassillis–Bargany feud, the Cathcarts sided with Bargany and Sir John Cathcart was actually with Gilbert when he was ambushed near Maybole. The Cathcarts also owned Killochan Castle three miles inland from Girvan.

Whether this Sir John is the same Sir John of legend and ballad is unclear. But whoever he was, this noble was a forerunner of Bluebeard in that he allegedly murdered seven brides for their dowries, before being beaten by a Kennedy lass.

Sir John Cathcart was courting May Culzean, a bonny lass with family connections to the lairds of Cassillis. He was a brave soldier, a fine looking man and rich to boot – so he seemed to be a good match for the ever-careful Kennedies. But the marriage negotiations were moving too slowly for the impatient swain and he convinced the fair May that they should run away together. So one night, dressed in all her finery and with a box of her mother's jewels tucked under her arm, she crept out of her home and into the arms of the waiting Sir John, looking forward to a life filled with love and passion. Sir John, however, had other ideas. He took her to a steep cliff to the south of Lendalfoot known as 'Games Loup' and told her, in the words of an old ballad:

DEVIL'S GALLOP

> Here I have drowned seven maids fair.
> The eighth one you shall be.

It seems he was more interested in obtaining jewels and finery than in settling down, so he told the young girl to take off her jewel-encrusted dress before he pushed her over. But May blushed and asked him:

> Oh turn ye about, Sir John
> And look to the leaf o' the tree.
> For it never became a gentleman
> A naked woman to see.

Sir John might have been a serial killer, but he was still a gentleman, so he turned as he was asked. May might have been a naïve lass but she was no fool. She began to take off her clothes before seizing her chance and pushing him over the cliff instead.

> Now lie there, thou faux Sir John,
> Where ye thocht to lay me.
> Although you see me stripped to the skin
> Your claes ye ha gotten wi' thee.

Games Loup rose on the left as I drove out of the far end of the village, just as I began to climb the road over Bennane Head. I was on the final stretch now – for this is where the Beane family called home.

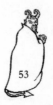

TEN

Neighbours From Hell

The road climbed steeply before swooping down the other side towards Ballantrae bay. The village and its harbour could be seen in the distance but I was not heading there just yet. At the foot of the hill, a road led off to the right. Clinging tenaciously to the side of the cliffs, this once formed part of the A77 until the new road diverted traffic over the hill. It is now an access road only, so I parked almost as soon as I turned into it and walked the rest of the way. This being part of a farm, nature is slowly reclaiming the concrete roadway so I was not surprised to come face-to-face with a cow nibbling at tufts of grass that are forcing their way through the tarmac. With that in mind, I ensured I closed all the gates – not forgetting to step gingerly, as cows have that charming habit of leaving mementoes of their visit – and I finally considered the full story of Sawney Beane.

Sawney (or Alexander) Beane was born, it is said, during the fourteenth century in East Lothian. His father was a hedger and ditcher, an honest man who believed in a good day's work. He tried to train his son in his trade but the younger Beane had no interest in honest toil, preferring to cut throats than hedges. So, hooking up with a woman of the streets who boasted the same nasty tendencies as himself, he set off for the West Coast and the lands of Carrick.

The couple soon found a cave on Bennane Head, which was ideal for their purposes. It had a narrow mouth that opened up a mile inside into a large cavern. Because it was a sea cave, they were safe from pursuit whenever the tide was in – that is if anyone could find it in the first place. It would be another 25 years before they visited a town or village again. During that time they bred prodigiously, begetting sons and daughters who went on to beget a further fearsome brood of children.

The Beanes lived by robbing and murdering unwary travellers. In the spirit of 'waste not want not', their victims were carried off, cut into quarters and pickled for when times were lean. Individual Meat Pie (ingredients: one individual) was a favourite treat at the Beane family table. Business was so good for the cannibals that their larder was often full to overflowing, forcing them to dispose of some of their comestibles by throwing them into the sea. The tides eventually washed the body parts ashore, naturally causing great alarm among the local populace. Fear was already rife in the area due to the number of mysterious disappearances; the discovery of limbs apparently hacked from the bodies sent further terror rippling through the citizenry.

No one knew the Beanes even existed. There were rumours of course, and stories to frighten children, but no one really knew there were real monsters lurking in the dark. And so paranoia set in. Honest travellers were arrested on suspicion of murder and wrongfully hanged. Innkeepers fell under suspicion because missing people spent final nights in their establishment. Many were lynched: others closed their inns and left the area. Meanwhile, the Beanes continued to live off their home-cooked Kate and Sidney Pie and the tides still delivered bits of flesh onto local beaches.

One day a man and woman were making their way home from a local fair, having grown tired of the 'coconute shie', the 'byngoe' and 'ye olde dodgems'. They picked their way through a nearby forest riding the same horse – the man in front, the woman behind. Naturally, they knew all about the disappearances but they knew such tragedies only affect other people. It would never happen to them.

The Beane clan ambushed them, leaping out from behind trees and rocks. They were a fearsome sight – clothed in rags, hair long and lank, skin matted with filth, nails long and talon-like, teeth sharp and snapping. The horse reared, throwing the woman from the saddle. The man drew his sword, hacking to the left and right, thrusting and slashing at the press of snarling bodies around him.

In a scene that would have had Italian horror film directors rubbing their hands together with glee, they fell on the woman like starving wolves. Her throat was ripped open as she hit the ground and her horrified husband could only watch as they 'fell to sucking her blood . . . as if it had been wine'. Then they clawed at her clothes, ripping them from her before tearing at her body until the flesh ruptured and they could drag her entrails forth to bite into them hungrily. Her husband might have gone the same way as his wife had a band of 20 men not arrived, causing the hideous bandits to melt off into the shadows.

The man was taken over 60 miles to Glasgow to tell his tale to magistrates. Those worthies sent word to the King in Edinburgh, who was so disturbed by the events that he personally led a cadre of 500 armed men to Carrick to hunt down and bring these creatures to justice. Again, the countryside resounded to the baying of bloodhounds as the search party roamed all over the territory, searching hill, dale, nook and cranny. But like many other search parties before them, they ignored the water-filled cave.

The dogs, however, knew better.

At the cave mouth they set up 'a most hideous barking, howling and yelping', and refused to leave. The King's men knew they would have to search the cave. At first they could see nothing in the darkness but convinced by the dogs straining at their leashes, they ventured further. Torches threw strange dancing shadows on the cold, wet walls as they stepped carefully into the gloom, the hounds still baying, the sounds echoing back and forth around them. Deeper and deeper into the cave they went, until finally the roof opened above them and they found themselves in a vast arched cavern. It was here they found the first trace of their quarry – and it was a sight they would remember for the rest of their days. All around them hung torsos stripped of limbs, hung in rows like carcasses in a butcher's shop. The arms and legs hung nearby, while barrels were filled with entrails, brains and eyes – all pickled and preserved like sweetmeats. Clearly, the Beane menu was not so much gourmet as goremet. The hunters also found a fortune in gold, silver and jewels, all stolen from victims. And then there were the Beanes themselves, spitting and snarling at their pursuers from the shadows – Sawney and his wife, eight sons, six daughters, 18 grandsons and 14 granddaughters. It seemed there had been quite bit of begetting over the years.

The King ordered the remains to be buried and the Beane brood to be taken back to Edinburgh where they were thrown into the tollbooth to await execution. There would be no trial, no lawyers pleading, no evidence lodged. The Beanes were guilty and by God they were to pay.

The males were disposed of first. They were dragged to Leith where their hands and feet were cut off. Then they were castrated before being hung on stakes to bleed slowly to death. Finally their corpses were thrown onto a huge fire and burned until only a powder remained. The Beane women were forced to witness the deaths of their men before they were burned at the stake in three separate fires. They died cursing their executioners and society at large, screaming and 'venting the most dreadful imprecations until the very last gasp of life'.

The story is a bloodthirsty one and first appeared in print around 1700 in the broadsheets, the tabloid newspapers of their day. There is, however, no actual record of the murders or the chase and certainly nothing about baked Beanes in Leith. As to which king led the hunt, even that is open to some doubt. Some accounts place it (as I have) during the reign of James I of Scotland (1394–1437) while others say it was James VI of Scotland (1566–1625). Among supporters of the latter possibility is S.R. Crockett, who includes Sawney and his brood in the general Kennedy skulduggery that makes up his book *The Grey Man*.

These days the cave is said to be below a former car park that can still be seen jutting off from the old road. They say a treacherous path leads down to the cove below, where a cleft in the rock marks the opening, although the majority of the cave was blocked off on the orders of King James, according to the tale. If you want – and are wearing some strong boots – you can try to find it. But for me, this was far enough. It was sufficient for me to stand in this disused car park with the sound of the waves crashing on the rocks below and the cries of the sea birds around me reminding me of the screams of the Beanes' victims. I know the cave exists; I know that Sawney and his family lived there; I know that a horrified king led a party of armed men with vengeance on their mind on a manhunt across this land. I do not need official records to tell me it is true. I do not need documents or testimony or eye-witness accounts. The story is all that matters and it is a good one.

Before I returned to Glasgow, I popped into Ballantrae. In the old churchyard I found the tomb of Sir Gilbert Kennedy. The Kennedy Mausoleum was built by his wife, Janet Stewart, and his body was interred here almost four years after his death, on 15 September 1605. His wife was also later buried beside him.

Also in Ballantrae is the last of our long line of Kennedy strongholds – Ardstinchar Castle. It was built in 1421 by Hugh Kennedy, who was originally studying for the priesthood but, being a Kennedy and therefore fond of a good Donnybrook, gave it all up to head off to France with 100 men to fight for the Dauphin in the 100 Years War. He was rewarded with a knighthood and some cash and on his return home he bought the lands of Ardstinchar for the princely sum of ten pounds. The castle is a ruin now – and a dangerous one at that, so I admired it from the road. Stones were taken from it to help build the nearby three-arched bridge.

Oh – and Mary Queen of Scots slept here in 1563. But she was a gal who slept around, so what else is new?

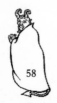

DEVIL'S GALLOP

BORDER RAID

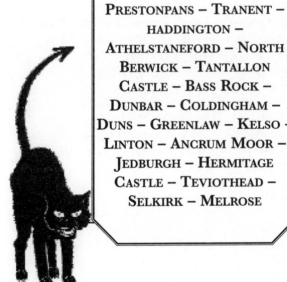

PRESTONPANS – TRANENT – HADDINGTON – ATHELSTANEFORD – NORTH BERWICK – TANTALLON CASTLE – BASS ROCK – DUNBAR – COLDINGHAM – DUNS – GREENLAW – KELSO – LINTON – ANCRUM MOOR – JEDBURGH – HERMITAGE CASTLE – TEVIOTHEAD – SELKIRK – MELROSE

ELEVEN

Witch Report

The thing about the M8 is it's so boring.

This occurred to me as I drove eastwards to begin my tour down the coast to the Borders. I know all motorways tend to the dull side but for me the main route between Glasgow and Edinburgh abuses the privilege. Perhaps it's because I've travelled on it so many times. Perhaps it's because I'm travelling so fast I don't have the time to take in any of the scenery. There is a very nice view around the turn-off to Shotts, but there are no scenic wonders on this road. Coal bings dot the landscape between Coatbridge and Livingston; silent memorials to a once prevalent industry, now reduced to ugly open-cast sites and I think only one deep mine.

The land around here was the haunt of robber Bertram de Shotts, who was hunted down and killed by John Muirhead. He chopped off Bertie's head and presented it to the king, who was so delighted that he gave him an estate and the right to have three acorns on his shield. One of the acorns represented the head, but I can only wonder what he cut off to deserve the other two.

The M8 ends at the outer reaches of Edinburgh and I followed the signs pointing to the A720, the city bypass. On my right rose the Pentland Hills, which gave their name to a tiny rebellion in 1666 when a force of Covenanters, incensed over the treatment of a farmer whom soldiers had tried to roast alive, marched from Galloway to Colinton to meet up with some like-minded folk. Unfortunately, the reinforcements failed to show and after sheltering from a blizzard in the kirkyard at Colinton they headed back home. On 28 November, that great tormentor of the Covenanters and staunch royalist Sir Tam Dalyell caught up with them at Rullion Green on the slopes of Turnhouse Hill. While the poorly equipped Covenanters sang psalms, the 3,000 experienced, battle-hardened regulars howled down upon them and turned the snow blood-red.

They say 100 Covenanters died on the hill (although the memorial high on the hills above the Flotterstone Inn off the A702 near Penicuik says it was 50). Three times that many were hunted down as they fled and were slaughtered by troops and even local peasants. Others were rounded up and marched to Edinburgh to be tried and executed. Royalist troops stripped the bodies but later Edinburgh women came out and wrapped them in shrouds of household linen and buried the men where they had fallen.

Eventually, I turned off the motorway onto the A199 to head for Prestonpans. Here, of course, Bonnie Prince Charlie caught the English General Sir John Cope with his trousers down and gave his troops a severe thrashing. To reach what is left of the battle site I followed the signs for Cockenzie before a road took me in the direction of Prestonpans. There is a sign pointing to the battlefield just at a monument marked, simply, 1745. I parked in the car park beside the East Lothian Indoor Bowling Club building, and another sign on the right directed me through the bushes to a pyramid shaped hill. At the top is the viewpoint-cum-memorial, where a series of plaques tells the story and points out various landmarks. Disappointingly, there is little left of the rough fields over which the Highlanders charged and the English fled. Much of it is taken up now with playing fields and industrial development.

Having eventually unfurled his banner at Glenfinnan in August 1745, Charles – the son of the 'Old Pretender' James – marched southwards. General Cope had literally tried to head him off at the pass – Corrieyarick of that ilk – but the Jacobites got there first, forcing Cope to retreat first to Inverness and then to Aberdeen to sail south.

Meanwhile, Charlie and his bickering generals had reached Edinburgh and although the Castle remained closed to them, they did occupy the city, where the young Prince set many an Edinburgh lady's heart a-flutter. Meanwhile Cope had landed at Dunbar and was determined to halt the Jacobite march south. On 19 September, he led his troops to this field in Prestonpans and awaited the arrival of the Highland army. He was well entrenched. The land around him was

DEVIL'S GALLOP

marshy and full of ditches and stone walls, while behind him was the Firth of Forth. 'Right,' you can almost hear him say, 'let's see Johnny Highlander get through that lot!'

But the Jacobites had a trump card – a local man called Robert Anderson who knew a path through the boggy ground. And so in the early hours of 21 September they were able to surge out of the morning mist and fall onto the government forces. The poorly-trained troops proved no match for charging Highlanders with the element of surprise and decades of pent-up fury behind them. The English line wavered, took another look at the oncoming kilted hellions, said something like, 'Bugger this for a game of soldiers' and fled. According to legend, Cope was asleep when the attack started – hence the Scots song 'Hey, Johnnie Cope, are ye wauken yet?' – and was the first to flee the scene. He had, however, been awake all night inspecting his troops, although he may well have been tucking into his rice crispies when the Highlanders came screaming out of the mist. During his retreat, he passed through Highland lines by placing a white cockade in his hat.

Meanwhile, the Jacobite Robertson of Struan, who had led his clan in battle, returned home to Perthshire in the General's own carriage. Familiar with the climate of those hills, he draped Cope's fur-lined nightgown around his aged shoulders.

One Royalist who did not reach the safety of England was General Gardiner, who lived at Bankend House, which can be seen from the monument. He was in command of a troop of dragoons who deserted the field at the earliest opportunity, leaving him wounded but still game for a scrap. He saw a group of leaderless infantrymen, and with a cry of 'Fire away men and fear nothing!' he galloped to help them. Eventually, though, he was cut down by a MacGregor axe, at a point on the field which was for a long time marked by a thorn tree. The brave general was carried up the slope to Tranent manse where it was found he had suffered two gunshot wounds and six slashes to the head. As he lay in the arms of the minister's niece, he asked for a sip of water, but died just as the cup was placed to his lips. Gardiner was buried in Tranent graveyard where his wife erected a monument that later disappeared. It is believed that it was used in 1799 to help form the walls of the new church.

DEVIL'S GALLOP

After the battle, orders went out for wounded redcoats to be fairly treated. One Highlander carried a bleeding trooper on his back to a place of safety and even left sixpence for his night's lodgings. Meanwhile, the Prince and his staff apparently set out tables on the battlefield and enjoyed a meal in honour of the brave Highlanders who had fought so well.

Looking towards Musselburgh and Edinburgh I could see the site of the earlier Battle of Pinkie. It is unlikely that the charging Highlanders who severely put the wind up the redcoats at Prestonpans (or Gladsmuir as some Scots called it) saw their victory as some form of payback for this 1547 slaughter but it would be poetic if they did.

The battle came towards the end of the so-called 'Rough Wooing', when Henry VIII wanted to marry the young Mary off to his sickly son Edward. The Scots, none too happy with this idea, were busy courting the French, which got right up the English noses. By September 1547 the old King was dead but the English Lord Protector, Somerset, decided to make a great foray north to bring the whole thing to a bloody conclusion. The two armies met around Inveresk, at the area known as Pinkie Cleugh. The Scots were ravaged by English artillery and guns blasted from a fleet anchored in the Firth of Forth while enemy cavalry mopped up the rest. As many as 10,000 Scots died on the banks of the little River Esk that day, while the English lost only 250 men. Somerset was able then to push on to Stirling where young Mary was being kept, although she was quickly spirited away to Inchmahome Priory on the Lake of Menteith (see Appin Way). Soon she was in France and well away from English hands.

Part of the Battle of Pinkie was fought on land now covered by Prestongrange Golf Course. In 1732, at Prestongrange House – now used by the Club Royal of Musselburgh – the Lord of Session, James Erskine (Lord Grange) informed friends that his dear wife had died. There was grieving, there was a funeral, there was his lordship walking behind the bier weeping like a baby. The only thing was, reports of his wife's death were somewhat exaggerated. She was at this time enjoying the dubious hospitality of some Highland caterans in a mountain hideaway. His lordship had decided she was mad and wanted her out of the way, so he arranged for her to be kidnapped from her Edinburgh lodgings. She was shipped off to barren St Kilda, and there she survived for seven years dependent on a local minister for shelter. (She might have been mad before all this, but by now she was really quite irked.) Finally, though, a letter got through to the Lord Advocate and she was brought back to the mainland. She died in 1745 on Skye. Surprisingly, no action was taken against her pious Presbyterian husband.

Leaving the battlesite, I headed up the hill to Tranent. One of the first coal mines in Scotland was dug here and during the Battle of Pinkie fearful locals took refuge in the mine workings but victorious English forces lit fires at the opening and suffocated them all.

There was more violence 350 years later when the government, worried over the revolution in France, decided to enforce the Militia Ballot Act in Scotland. They had calculated they needed 6,000 men to keep the peace should the French desire for liberty, equality and fraternity raise its head here. The Scots were slow to sign up so the authorities decided that single men aged between 19 and 23 could be balloted for service – unless, of course, they had the money to pay for someone else to stand in as a substitute. Riots ensued as Scots protested over being caught in the draft and Tranent was the scene of the most famous of these.

The men here were miners – hard, tough men; men not afraid of a fight but who felt they provided enough for the country by working in the deep pit with just a candle for light and their backs bent and broken by the heavy weights they had to carry. On 29 August 1797, the mob in the High Street rose up in defiance and tried to present a petition to the ballot officers. Soldiers and cavalry were sent out and they attacked the protesters, who were following local lass Jackie Crookston as she beat a drum and led the 'No Militia' cry. At least 11 people were killed as the military ran amok, shooting and hacking indiscriminately at the locals as they fled into fields around the town. They say some bodies remained missing until harvest time. Jackie Crookston was one of the dead and today a statue of her beating her drum and calling for liberty stands in Civic Square, just off High Street. Unfortunately, all it says at the base of the statue is her name and the year 1797, so the casual visitor would have no idea what it all means.

Mary Queen of Scots here makes her first appearance in this tour, in an episode which shows one of two things – either she was complicit in the murder of her husband Lord Darnley or she was so afraid of Bothwell, who would become her third hubby, that she did not show any grief. Two days after Darnley's death, she visited Seton Castle and played golf on the links – making her the first recorded woman golfer. She also won an archery contest with Bothwell and other nobles. The losers came to a Tranent inn afterwards and treated her to a dinner.

It was a baillie of Tranent, David Seaton, who sparked off the infamous North Berwick witch trials. In 1590, he grew suspicious over his servant Geillis Duncan's ability to heal the sick, believing she was in league with the Devil. She denied the charge of course, but that wasn't enough for Master Seaton so he resorted to the use of certain devices . . .

'Pilniewinks' and 'Bootikins' sound like characters from Beatrix Potter's books, or a song from *Cats*. They were, however, instruments of torture. The pilniewinks were a near relation to thumbscrews (or 'thumbiekins', as they were so cutely called in Scotland) except they crushed *all* the fingers of one hand. Geillis Duncan was subjected to this. She also had her head 'thrawed' (tied tightly in a rope that was twisted violently). Throughout it all, she refused to confess. However, when a search was made of her body and the Devil's Mark – a spot impervious to pain – was found on her throat, she admitted to being a witch.

But the investigations did not stop there, for the serving-girl had implicated others in her Devil's brood, including local schoolteacher Dr John Cunningham (or 'Fian'), midwife Agnes Sampson and a host of other women – including some of the great and the good. Sampson is perhaps the best known and she was tortured into confessing by the use of the 'witches' bridle', a device with sharp prongs that were forced into the mouth against the tongue and cheeks. She was thrawed and deprived of sleep. Cunningham was subjected to the bootikins, which involved the foot being jammed into a box, and wedges driven in until the bones were crushed. In his case, the torture went on until the 'blood and marrow spouted forth in great abundance'. He also had his fingernails pulled off by 'torkas' (a set of pincers), and nails thrust into the flesh of his fingertips. Naturally, he agreed to everything his questioners accused him of, hoping that confession would be good for his sole . . .

King James VI took a special interest in the proceedings. His mother, Mary, had introduced the first law banning witchcraft and he thought the practice a 'synne most odious'. This paranoid, suspicious little man even wrote a book on the subject, *Daemonologie*, which became a kind of self-help book for would-be witch hunters throughout the seventeenth century.

It was alleged that Agnes Sampson and her coven had plotted to kill both the King and his new wife, Anne of Denmark. While being 'put to the question' (a polite way of saying they were tortured into saying anything) the women claimed to have met with the Devil in North Berwick kirkyard where, by use of magic, they conjured up a storm to wreck the royal ship. The crossing from Denmark had been remarkably rocky and this was taken as corroboration of the charge!

According to the confessions, the Devil took them to sea and told them to throw a cat into the water, the cat having previously been drawn across a fire nine times (one for each life, obviously). This supposedly caused a tremendous tempest designed to drown the royal couple. This having been done, the coven returned to the kirk, led by Geillis Duncan playing the Jew's harp – the sound of which fairly tickled the King when he heard it in court. (All they needed was Lee Marvin and they could have put on a production of *Paint Your Wagon*.) After a quick snack on a corpse or two, the Devil had them 'caussit to kiss his erse'. Those who puckered up to deliver a big, wet one on Satan's fleshy parts said they were 'cauld lyk yce'. (So would yours be if you'd dropped your kegs above the Firth of Forth in a wind sharp enough to shave a minister.) They also described 'his body hard lyk yrn; his faice was terrible; his nose lyk the bek of ane egle; gret handis and feit lyk the griffon, and spak with a low voice'. Aye – and pygs micht flie!

But if all this was not enough, the inquisitors took the conspiracy a step further – for the witches then implicated Francis, Earl of Bothwell in their plot, claiming he was the warlock who led them! The fact that James didn't care much for Bothwell, whom he saw as a threat, did not influence the inquisitors at all. Bothwell was charged and imprisoned in Edinburgh Castle, but he managed to escape.

66 **DEVIL'S GALLOP**

It has been estimated that about 70 persons in all were eventually accused of witchcraft during this period. Many were executed – strangled then burned – including John Cunningham, Geillis Duncan and Agnes Sampson.

From Tranent I followed the signs for Macmerry, before making for Haddington.

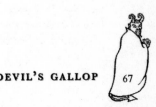

TWELVE

The Rock

Once I had found somewhere to park in Haddington, I made my way on foot to St Mary's Kirk on the banks of the Tyne. This river has proved to be something of a worry for the inhabitants over the centuries, having burst its banks on many occasions. The town was saved once by divine intervention, when a nun threatened to throw a statue of the Virgin Mary into the water unless it receded. (It did, making this a case virgin on the miraculous.)

Haddington has been burned, sacked and generally discommoded many times. King John put a light to it in 1216 and again two years later. Edward III watched it burn in 1355. Henry IV visited in 1400 but kept his Swan Vestas in his pocket. In 1598 it was again burned, not this time by an invading army but by a servant drying clothes too near to an open fire.

The most notable event here was the siege of 1548–49, during the 'Rough Wooing'. A parliament had been convened in the Abbey where the French and Scottish governments agreed that young Mary should marry the French Dauphin when they were both of age. Later that year, the English took the town and fortified it before the Scots turned up outside crying, 'Siege you, Jimmy!'

According to one account, the English garrison repulsed assaults and led many a successful sally. (I don't know what she was successful at but whatever it was, the Scots couldn't get a toehold.) Eventually, plague did what the Scots armies could not and the garrison had to be relieved after 18 months when an English general managed to sneak into the town and spirit the remaining soldiers away to Berwick. And so ended the longest siege of any British town.

It was during this time that the magnificent abbey-cum-church of St Mary's was almost destroyed. The roof was burned and not replaced until the 1970s. It is a quite incredible building for what is apparently a simple parish church and well worth a look.

On leaving Haddington, crossing the bridge over the Tyne, I made my way onto the A1, turning towards Berwick-upon-Tweed. Ahead of me and to my right I saw Trapain Law, the great humpbacked hill that played an influential role in the story of Glasgow's patron saint. 'Law' in old Scots means 'hill'. In the east we have North Berwick Law, Duns Law and Scald Law, among others. Centuries ago, Trapain Law was the capital of the Votadini people whose King Loth gave his name to Lothian. Loth had a daughter, Thenew, who found herself in a delicate condition after an encounter with a Welsh prince (or at least, that's how one version of the story tells it). Her father was beside himself and demanded to know who the lass had been going horizontal jogging with. She refused to tell him so he had her thrown from the top of the Law into the sea. Even an idle glance at a map will tell you that it was a throw of Olympic proportions. Old Loth no doubt paraphrased the words of the late great Reggie Bosanquet when he thought, 'Well, that's the end of Thenew.' But he was wrong, for his daughter drifted into the Firth of Forth, eventually washing up on the north bank of the river near Culross (see Rebel March).

From the A1, I turned left at a sign for Athelstaneford, where Scotland first adopted the St Andrew's Cross as its national flag.

According to legend the Saxon monarch Aethelstane fought here with a combined Pict–Scots force under Kings Hungus and Achaius around AD 832. Before the battle, as was the custom, the home side prayed to God to give them the strength to slaughter their foes. God sent a sign that he was with them – a giant white 'X' against a blue sky. St Andrew became the patron saint of Scotland, while the saltire became the symbol of Scotland and as such is said to be the oldest in Europe.

In the grounds of the parish church there is a memorial with a battle scene carved in granite. An old doocot behind the church has been turned into a small heritage centre and the ground around it acts as a vantage point to view the supposed site of the battle near the Peffer Burn. As my luck would have it, the centre was closed the day I visited.

I continued on the meandering country road to North Berwick, where I parked near the harbour. Beside the modern RSPB Centre overlooking the water, I found what little was left of the old kirkyard where the witches danced. Only a few very low walls remain which unfortunately fail to give any impression of what the medieval building was like. Even the graveyard where the witches once dined on human flesh is gone.

However, there is a large Celtic cross nearby which stimulated my imagination. It is dedicated to Catherine Watson, a Glasgow art student, who was drowned in the east bay in July 1889 while rescuing a drowning boy. As I stood there looking at the memorial erected by grateful locals, I wondered who this girl was, why she was here and what her life was like. For some reason, thoughts of Kate Watson lingered with me as I left North Berwick and headed along the coast towards Tantallon Castle.

It was a bright, crisp, autumn day and the view here was stunning. The castle rose out of the land and towered seaward, red and forbidding, looking every inch the medieval stronghold, protected on three sides by water and on the fourth by earthworks and fortifications. Just beyond it stood the craggy lump of stone that is the Bass Rock, its top frosted with seabirds. One writer said the castle frowns across the water at the Bass and never a truer word was written.

They say MacDuff, Thane of Fife and nemesis of Shakespeare's *Macbeth*, once held it, although work on the present structure did not begun until the mid-fourteenth century. It was then held by the Douglases of Angus (known as the Red Douglases) – and that lot needed somewhere impregnable to scamper to when their many intrigues and plots brought them trouble. Thanks to their antics, Tantallon has been under siege a number of times. In 1491, the fifth Earl, Archibald Douglas, was getting altogether too cosy with England's Henry VII so James IV blockaded the castle. Everything ended amicably enough though, and Archibald died in his bed over 20 years later.

His grandson, also named Archibald (the Douglases had as much imagination when it came to names as the Kennedies of Ayrshire) got himself hitched to Margaret Tudor, widow of James IV and (funnily

DEVIL'S GALLOP

enough) mother of James V, and formed part of a rota of nobles who were to take care of the young king. But in 1525, he refused to part with the teenage monarch and kept him prisoner in Edinburgh Castle for the next two and a half years. Eventually, James escaped and had Archibald put to the horn (basically outlawed with his lands and goods forfeit to the crown, which was always a good way for the Stewart kings to raise a bit of folding green). James then raised an army and marched on Tantallon where Archibald had dug in. And as the royal drummer rattled out 'Ding Doun Tantallon', the cannons blasted at the walls. For 20 days they roared but Tantallon still stood.

The following year, with Archibald in exile, James finally took possession of the castle. But by 1543 the Earl was back – and still up to his neck in politics. He took Henry's side during the Rough Wooing, even storing the treasure with the English king to bribe those Scottish nobles who were always open to financial inducement. However in 1545, Archibald suffered a severe attack of patriotism and helped lead the Scottish forces to victory at Ancrum Moor (more on this later). His change of heart, they say, was caused by the English desecration of Douglas tombs at Melrose Abbey. In 1556, the sixth Earl, like his granddad, died peacefully at home.

There was a brief intermission in the Archibalds when David Douglas took the title, but he died in 1557, leaving a two-year-old child to fill the void. Just for a change, his name was Archibald, and as soon as he was old enough he started playing up to the English, just like his forefathers. He spent a year in exile then retired to Tantallon, intending to live out the rest of his life in peace and quiet. However, that was not to be, for in 1588 he died of a mysterious disease attributed to the 'black arts' of his wife, Barbara Napier, one of the 'North Berwick witches'. She escaped execution by 'pleading her belly' – she was pregnant and was eventually set free.

The final act of defiance at Tantallon took place in 1650–51 when a small band of Covenanters used it as a base to raid Cromwell's supply lines and General Monck was despatched with a force of 2,000–3,000 men to capture them. For 12 days the 91 men held off the superior attacking forces, until they finally retreated to the tower where they resolved to fight and die. But the Roundheads recognised courage when they saw it and showed mercy.

DEVIL'S GALLOP

Across the water, the Bass Rock has a strong Covenanter connection, for many a pious prisoner was sent to this inhospitable lump of lava when it was turned into a prison in 1651. Conditions were frightful and many prisoners died. Rain and snow provided fresh water and the prisoners had to supply their own food. One Edinburgh tollbooth inmate found himself Bass bound after doctors announced he needed fresh air – and the air doesn't get much fresher than at the mouth of the Forth.

The stories of the Covenanter captives are horrendous, but it is a group of later prisoners who provide some romance.

In 1691, four Jacobites took possession of the prison by locking their guards out of the building while they were landing coal. Soon, other like-minded adventurers joined the prisoners and together they waged a small war on the outside world, seizing fishing boats and demanding ransoms for their return. The navy tried to put a stop to this piracy but the Bass was too well fortified and the buccaneer brotherhood – all 16 of them – had too many supporters on the mainland, who helped keep them supplied.

They held out for three years, refusing to budge even when the brother of one of their number was strung up on a gibbet near Tantallon. Finally, in April 1694, they left the Bass for exile in France. The government, wishing rid of this small force that had embarrassed them for so long, granted them safe passage.

I wished I had had more time to spend here. The sun was shining, the sea was blue, and the Bass (now a bird sanctuary) looked almost inviting. But I had other sights to see. Heading back to the A1, I passed through the tiny village of Whitekirk. The small St Mary's Kirk here was founded in the seventh century by St Baldred and there is a legend that an invading English soldier tried to steal a ring from a statue of the Virgin Mary but was stopped by a spiritual slap on the wrist – a crucifix fell on the said wrist and broke it. Later, the ship that sailed away with the booty sank in the mouth of the River Tyne nearby. That'll teach them.

THIRTEEN

The Long March

Dunbar Castle dates from the eleventh century and there is not much now to suggest the vital importance of this stronghold to both the Scots and the English. Dunbar was on the main route from the south to Edinburgh, allowing the land armies to remain in contact with any fleet sailing in support. Edward II fled here after Bannockburn to take a ship and scuttle south to think again. General Cope landed here before his fateful breakfast meeting with the Highlanders at Prestonpans.

In 1339, the English returned to Dunbar. The Scots were – again – without an adult monarch and Edward III was using the confusion to interfere in the affairs of his northern neighbour. Edward Balliol, son of John Balliol, had seized the throne after his army (including disinherited Scottish nobles once banished by the Bruce) beat the forces of the Regent Mar at Dupplin Moor. Once crowned at Scone he headed south, but another Scots force caught him at Annan and drove him across the border to his English friends. Archibald Douglas was named Regent but everything came unstuck at Halidon Hill, near Berwick, when the Scots forces withered and died under hails of English arrows. Meanwhile, the young King David (Bruce's son) was carried off to safety in France.

Over the next few years many people tried to wrest the crown of Scotland from Balliol's head but he had Edward behind him. During one such attempt, the Earl of Salisbury laid siege to Dunbar Castle (like Tantallon protected on three sides by water) but found himself stymied by a woman – Black Agnes Randolph, so called because of her shock of dark hair. She was as spirited as she was beautiful, and when Salisbury demanded her surrender she gave him a verbal two fingers and settled in for siege. For six months the English pressed and blasted at the walls but were held off by Black Agnes's defiant leadership and snook-cocking. As the cannons roared, she had maidservants rush out to clean off the dust raised from the walls with linen cloths. She had an apparent traitor lure the Earl and his men to the open gates but Salisbury smelled a rat. He held back and a servant went under the gates, which clanged down behind him. On another occasion the Earl was inspecting his troops when an arrow darted from the battlements and killed a man beside him. 'The Countess's love arrows pierce to the heart,' he remarked.

Finally though, Scottish reinforcements sailed down the coast, dodged Salisbury's ships blockading the harbour, and relieved the castle. Black Agnes is remembered in the name of a pub in the town.

Dunbar Castle also has connections with another woman – the ubiquitous Mary Queen of Scots. She came here with Darnley after the murder of her secretary David Rizzio in Holyrood. She was heavily pregnant at the time and the news that her husband had changed sides (having been part of the conspiracy to murder the little Italian) sent some of his erstwhile partners ducking for cover.

Later it was to Dunbar that Bothwell brought the Queen after seizing her at Bridge of Almond, to the west of the capital. They say he raped her here. They say she fell in love with him. The only thing that is certain, though, is that she married the dashing (but some might say homicidal) Earl. But Mary's affections were as changeable as the Scottish weather. Her marriage to Bothwell a mere three months after Darnley's death at Kirk o' Field was to prove her downfall. As things grew hot for the couple, critics began to believe she had been party to Darnley's murder, and the newly-weds again fled to Dunbar for what was to be their last night together. Bothwell's forces met the opposition at Carberry Hill, near Musselburgh. The couple were separated – Mary began her imprisonment, Bothwell tried to gather more support. Bothwell failed to find his backing and fled to Denmark, where he ended his days in prison, said to be quite mad. Gangrene from a wound eventually killed him, turning his body into a putrefying mess. His head, however, remained quite presentable – a fact not lost on the governor of the prison, who placed it on the disease-free body of an English agent who had come a cropper during an attempt on Bothwell's life. The mummified remains were put on

DEVIL'S GALLOP

display until they finally decayed due to poor storage and were placed in a closed coffin.

In military history circles, Dunbar is famous for two battles, although neither of them was fought in the town. The first took place in 1296 when John Balliol was defying his puppet-master Edward Plantagenet. Longshanks had sacked Berwick (then a Scottish port) and had sent his men up the coast to take Dunbar Castle and hold it. The English faced a Scottish army at Spott Burn, just over two miles south of the town. Like many another battle, it proved disastrous for Scotland as its army was hopelessly outclassed by the invaders.

The second clash came in 1650 when a Covenanting force, loyal by this time to Charles II, met Cromwell's army at Doon Hill (close to the site of the Edwardian battle). Under the leadership of David Leslie, the Scots had previously managed to give the Parliamentary forces a bloody nose at Leith. Cromwell, his men suffering from hunger and sickness as the Scottish scorched earth policy took hold, was returning south to Dunbar to lick his wounds and hopefully return home on the ships anchored there. The Scots could have let them leave but Leslie's religious masters were having none of it. They had already purged their own forces of the ungodly (unfortunately, including many of their most experienced soldiers); now they wanted Leslie to smite the enemy hip and thigh. God, after all, was with them and would not be happy until every English soldier lay maimed and bleeding on this sacred soil. They ordered Leslie to come down from his (stronger) position on Doon Hill.

Frankly, these religious maniacs should have kept their noses in the Good Book and out of the Military Manual. Cromwell, who had been praying for such a miracle, decided the best form of defence was attack. With the cry, 'Put your trust in God, my boys – and keep your powder dry,' he launched an offensive – even though he was outnumbered by more than two to one. The Scots, not expecting such a bold act from a demoralised army, their *own* powder wet from having spent a night on the damp hillside, were caught on the hop. Over 3,000 Scots were left dead on the field. Another 10,000 surrendered.

Half the prisoners were released on parole but the others were pushed south, on what was to be called the 'Durham Death March'. There were not enough provisions to keep them fed during the 118-

mile trek, even though civilians took pity and threw them food. Water, though, was obtained from muddy ditches and puddles. But still they fell. Around 1,500 perished on the road to Durham from hunger, sickness, thirst and infections.

Once in the English city, the survivors were herded into the cathedral which ten years before their countrymen had looted and vandalised. Cromwell's generals believed supplies were being sent for the prisoners' care, but the Parliamentary rank and file were stealing everything they could – while the Scots were dying at a rate of 30 a day. Of the 5,000 men who began the march, only 1,400 were still alive two months later. Many were sold into slavery in the Americas; others were sent off to fight for foreign powers. The ones who didn't make it were thrown into an unmarked mass grave in the cathedral grounds.

There is a monument to the battle just over two miles south of Dunbar. To find it I drove through the town onto the A1087, heading for Berwick. The stone is on the left-hand side of the road, within sight of the A1.

Near Dunbar is the village of Spott, once the home of a religious leader who would have fitted in well with the bloodthirsty Covenanter preachers. The Reverend John Kello thought he was destined for great things, if only he could off-load his wife, who he felt was keeping him back. He first tried (unsuccessfully) to poison her but then opted for a more hands-on approach. On 24 September 1570, he throttled the poor woman then tied a noose around her neck and hanged her to make it look like suicide. That done, he preached a sermon in the village before inviting two parishioners home to help him 'discover' the body. He himself went to the gallows a month later after confessing to the crime.

Heading south on the A1. I reached the turn-off to Coldingham, the A1107. This village takes some time to reach (it's easily one of the longest 12-mile stretches I've ever been on) but the visit to the priory here is worth it. Once in the village, I parked near the town hall and the priory entrance. The ruins here are all that remains of a twelfth century building which now forms part of the village church. However, there has been a religious presence here since the seventh century.

DEVIL'S GALLOP

The priory was besieged in 1537, and over 20 years later became home to 6,000 English soldiers. During the Civil War what was left of the building was taken over by Royalists, while the Commonwealth troops set up an artillery battery on a nearby hill and blasted them out with a two-day barrage.

But the story that interested me took place long before all this blood and thunder — when the east coast was forever being menaced by those hard-drinking, tough-loving, long-haired Norsemen. In those days there was a nunnery here and on one occasion the Mother Superior heard that Vikings were on their way with some slap and tickle in mind. To dampen the men's ardour a bit, she ordered all the nuns to cut off their noses. If that wasn't enough, she also told them to slice off their bottom lips. Just to set the tone, she did it first. Their self-mutilation had the desired effect, for the randy raiders were so repulsed by the sight of the nuns' faces that they burned the place down — with the ladies inside.

From Coldingham I headed inland. I was now in the border country.

FOURTEEN
Border Warfare

For centuries the borderland was the frontier for both Scots and English and was just as lawless as the old American West. The families who lived here generally showed little loyalty to either kingdom – for instance, when Scottish troops retreated from the debacle of Solway Moss, Borderers swooped down on them to rob and kill. Family loyalty was the most important thing here. The Armstrongs, Nixons, Humes, Scotts and all the other families who rampaged round this countryside were as clannish as any Highlander – and just as bloodthirsty. The blood feud was a way of life and each family would regularly raid the other, irrespective of which side of the national divide they lived. Cattle were lifted, homes were burned and people were slaughtered when these bands of raiders (or 'reivers' to give them their proper name) galloped down the valleys.

These fighting moss troopers (to give them another name) have left their mark on the countryside. The land is peppered with fortifications: castles and peel towers jut aggressively from moorland and hilltop, daring any English raider or Scottish king to test their mettle. At Greenknowe Tower, for instance, built by the Seton family, you can see the staircase winding clockwise to free the right-handed defenders' sword arms while their opponents had the wall impeding theirs. (The Kerr family, whose area was further south, were said to have a tendency to build their staircases anti-clockwise because they were notoriously left-handed – hence the expression 'Kerr-handed' or 'corry-fisted', as George MacDonald Fraser explains in his excellent book *The Steel Bonnets*.)

The lands alongside the border were split into six different territories (or 'marches') – three on each side. I was then in the Scottish East March. Later I would travel around the Scottish Middle

March. The Scottish West March was (unsurprisingly) further to the west, around Dumfries and the Solway Firth. Then there were the 'Debatable Lands', areas traversing the border where people held no allegiance to any family, or country.

In a bid to bring some sort of order, the respective governments appointed wardens to each of the marches. But the system of appointment was corrupt and did not work. The powerful families defied the orders of the Wardens, who were often following their own agenda anyway.

Following the B6438 from Coldingham, I crossed the A1 and, passing through the tiny settlements of Reston and Marygold, joined the A6112, turning left towards Duns. This land is known as the 'Merse'. Rich and fruitful, the farms around here were known as 'the storehouse of Scotland'. Even now you can see why families on both sides of the border fought over it hungrily, for the fertile ground would ensure prosperity for whoever controlled it.

Duns is a little town of narrow streets and dark stone houses that was destroyed and rebuilt three times during the turbulent years of the Scottish–English Wars. According to one story, its motto, 'Duns Dings A', goes back to the time when the local people filled animal skins with stones and used to create a 'dinging' noise to scare off English marauders. (If only Bruce and Wallace had known the English were frightened of an awful noise, they could have won Stirling and Bannockburn with the aid of some accordion music.)

It was near here in 1516 that a band of Humes, the most powerful family in the East March, hunted down Frenchman Anthony Darcy, who had been unfortunate enough – or stupid enough – to become Warden of *all* the Scottish Marches. He had been implicated in various political shenanigans that had led to the execution of the third Baron Hume and his brother in Edinburgh, so naturally he was not at the top of the family's Christmas card list. Coming upon him at Broomhouse, east of Duns, they chopped off his head and galloped off to their fortress with it tied by the hair to a saddle. His body was buried where he died and a monument raised here to commemorate the incident.

Over 100 years later, a Covenanting army almost met head-to-head with Royalist forces on Duns Law but for once hostilities were avoided. A large boulder, known as the Covenanters' Stone, is said to lie where General Leslie raised his standard but bits of it have been chipped away over the centuries leaving it a shadow of what it once was. Also, nearby is a monument to this military non-event.

In 1792 there was a riot here, when the populace objected strenuously to the new 'Turnpike Act' (which saw many tolls being levied on certain roads). Like many Acts, it was worded strongly in favour of the landed gentry who would receive a cut of the cash taken. Locals destroyed new tollgates and were imprisoned for their trouble. Some were even transported.

Later, there was another display of civil disobedience here, this time involving those enterprising businessmen 'the body snatchers' who felt it their duty to keep struggling doctors busy with fresh corpses for dissection. In 1825, a Duns innkeeper and a farmer friend startled two such likely lads while they were transporting a corpse, freshly dug up from a local kirkyard. The snatchers had placed the cadaver (of a man called MacGall) between them on their cart. When the innkeeper and chum challenged them, they leapt off the cart and disappeared into the night. The body was placed in Duns church and the vehicle left in the keeping of the town council. Later, a band of angry townspeople stole the cart and burned it in the town square. The council read the Riot Act – which prohibited gatherings of 12 or more people if they were behaving 'riotously and tumultuously'. This Act also allowed the authorities to shoot to kill if the assembly did not disperse within an hour. In this case the council refrained from ordering a massacre. The crowd dispersed when the cart was reduced to ashes.

Moving on from this picturesque town, I came to the village of Polworth. This is the site where in 1684, a young girl's bravery was demonstrated in helping her fugitive father. Covenanter Sir Patrick Hume was on the run from dragoons and for a time hid in his family's burial plot in the village's old churchyard. Every night his 18-year-old daughter Grisell brought him food, often walking past files of soldiers. Sir Patrick later hid in a specially dug hole near his home until he and his family were able to escape to the Netherlands.

Next I reached Greenlaw, where what looks like a tower built onto the kirk was actually a gaol. Built in 1700, it was known as the 'Hell's Hole', or 'Thieves' Hole', and was used to incarcerate prisoners until

DEVIL'S GALLOP

1829. Two years later, though, the body of robber Mannus Swinney was placed in the tower after he was hanged at the gibbet in the High Street in front of the Castle Inn hotel.

There is also a story told here of a witch who was being dragged off to be burned in a field just outside the town called Gallow's Lea. She asked for some water to which someone shouted, 'Don't let her drink – the drier she is, the better she'll burn.'

Continuing onwards, I turned right onto the B6364 and headed towards Kelso. It was on this road that I found the remains of Hume Castle, looking every inch the traditional fortress on its small hill beside the village, its sharp battlements squaring off against the sky. Unfortunately, it's not the original castle. That was destroyed and this one built centuries later out of the rubble.

For centuries, the most powerful family of the East March kept vigil from this vantage point, holding off an English force in 1548–49 and forcing them to vent their frustration on the surrounding countryside. The castle did fall about 20 years later, when Elizabeth sent her army, under the Earl of Sussex, north to punish the Scots for previous incursions into England and to stop any further talk of her cousin Mary taking the English throne. The castle was besieged and after murderous artillery fire the garrison was ordered to surrender by Lord Hume. For once there was no wholesale slaughter for the defenders were allowed to leave, although two English traitors were handed over for execution.

And so to Kelso, a charming market town with its elegant stone houses and its ruined abbey. The fact that the English gutted the abbey on more than one occasion will by now come as no surprise (after all, the Scots were doing the same to abbeys and churches across the border. It was the thing to do in the days before telly). In 1460, James III was crowned here, after his father was killed when a cannon called The Lion exploded beside him during a siege of Roxburgh Castle nearby.

In 1545, when the English came north on a burning spree, led by Edward Seymour, Earl of Hertford, Kelso found itself under attack – and not for the first time. The army comprised mainly foreign mercenaries and this time the monks of the abbey fought back. But when the English guns breached the abbey walls, the monks and

DEVIL'S GALLOP

townspeople – 102 in total – retreated to the tower resolving to hold out until the bitter end. That bloody, heroic end came the following day when the tower was taken and the defenders of this Scottish Alamo were slaughtered to a man.

In 1745, Bonnie Prince Charlie arrived with his army on his triumphant way south. The Prince stayed at the forerunner of today's Cross Keys Inn in the town's spacious square. The town showed him hospitality but did not provide any recruits.

Kelso is an ideal base from which to explore the surrounding countryside. From here for instance you can take the A699 to the ruins of Roxburgh Castle. There is not much to show of the castle that was at one time one of the most important in Scotland. King David I based his court here and it was deemed so significant that James II personally led the army to besiege it – and came a cropper when that cannon malfunctioned. The English also held Alexander III captive here.

The most notable tale, though, comes from 1313 when one of Robert the Bruce's closest friends, Sir James (the 'Black Douglas') resolved to wrest the fortress from English hands. He and 60 hand-picked black-clad men scaled the walls under cover of darkness until they reached the uppermost battlements. There, according to legend, a woman was soothing her child with the lullaby:

> Hush ye, hush ye, little pet ye
> Hush ye, hush ye, do not fret ye,
> The Black Douglas will not get ye.

Douglas reached out gently with his hand, touched the woman's shoulder and said, 'I wouldna be too sure of that.' The woman and her child came to no harm but the soldiers in the castle were slaughtered.

Leaving Kelso behind I took the B6436, following the signs for Yetholm and later those for Morebattle. My objective now was to find the small hamlet of Linton – in particular its church, which lies down a lane to the right of the road. Unfortunately, the sign pointing to the church was obscured by foliage and I missed it. It wasn't until I rounded a bend that I chanced to look back and saw the church and its

DEVIL'S GALLOP

attractively haphazard graveyard standing on a hillock. I was actually glad I had missed it because it was quite a sight from this part of the road.

Centuries ago, this area was plagued by a fearsome creature known as the Linton Wyrm that lived in a cave a mile to the south-east of the church and had a tendency to eat whatever came its way. Some say it was a dragon; some say it was a large serpent-like creature. The locals had tried to kill it several times but the beastie had bested them all.

'Oh, who will rid us of this monster?' cried the locals and up stepped John Somerville, tall of stature, broad of shoulder and mighty of bicep.

'I will slay your dragon,' he said, flashing them a Burt Lancaster grin. 'I will tackle it alone, with only ane stoute servant for company.'

And so, the gallant John rode out to face the monster, armed with a lance and some pieces of peat dipped in pitch and brimstone (sulphur). These medieval wyrm tablets were set alight and when the creature, (or 'dragoune') slithered from its lair, the knight rammed them deep into her throat. For good measure he stabbed the beastie with his broken lance. The dying wyrm wrapped its coils around the hill, which became known as 'Wormeston', and its agonised contractions left deep indentations in the land.

According to the legend, King William the Lion knighted the brave man and ordered that a stone be cut to immortalise the deed. This can still be seen above the door of the church, although the detail is very faint and it is now protected against the elements by a sheet of thick plastic. Naturally, there is some doubt about the truth of the tale. The Somerville family do have a symbolic dragon on their crest but no one is sure if it was there before the alleged wyrming.

On leaving Linton, I continued down the road until I reached a junction where I turned right through Morebattle. I was now following signs for Jedburgh and after a few miles I turned left onto the A698. As I drove through this fine agricultural country, I saw a stone column thrusting upwards from a hill to the right. This is the Waterloo Monument, built in 1815 to commemorate Wellington's victory. This area has a special attachment to that particular battle because many French POWs were brought here.

From here I took a detour, turning right where the A698 joins the

A68, following signs for St Boswells. I soon came to a sign pointing left to the tiny village of Ancrum. It was two miles north of here on 27 February 1545 that the Scots, under Sir Archibald Douglas, the sixth Earl of Angus, routed the English under Sir Ralph Eure and Sir Brian Laiton. This was during the Rough Wooing and Angus had recently changed sides – only three years before he had had his wrists slapped at Hadden Rigg while fighting for Henry VIII's team. (This should not be surprising for he was, after all, Henry's brother-in-law.)

At Ancrum Moor, the Scots were goaded on to victory by their belief that the English had burned alive an elderly woman and her family in a tower at Broomhouse. During the battle, some Scottish border families fighting under the English banner saw the way the wind was blowing and did what they did best – switched sides. The English troops – a motley crew from down south and the continent – discarded their armour and weapons to flee across the moor, pursued by angry locals who meted out some harsh justice.

Both English commanders died on the battlefield and were subsequently interred in Melrose Abbey, which ironically they had earlier burned. As the Regent Arran and Angus walked among the bodies strewn across the field after the battle, they found the corpse of Sir Ralph Eure, who, as Warden of the English Middle March, was much hated in Scotland. 'God have mercy on him, for he was a fell cruel man,' said Arran. Angus, himself no weak sister, nodded sagely.

Tradition states that a local woman called Lilliard joined the Scottish forces here to avenge the death of her lover at the hands of the English troops. She fought bravely, suffering many bloody wounds, including the loss of both her legs. But she was a game girl, was Lilliard, for she continued to fight on her stumps until she was finally killed. There is a stone marking the spot where she was buried (called, fittingly, Lilliard's Edge) about 200 metres from the main road on the way to St Boswell's. To reach it, I parked in a lay-by near to a caravan site and walked along the road up the hill. I turned through a gate at the summit and followed a farm track until I reached the grave. There are some fine views from here – to the right, over the battlefield and to the left, across to the triple peaks of the Eildon Hills.

But all too soon I had to make my way back to the car and drive back down the A68 to reach Jedburgh.

DEVIL'S GALLOP

FIFTEEN

Hang Now, Ask Questions Later

Once in the town, I parked midway between the ruined abbey and the house (now a museum) where Mary Queen of Scots reputedly found herself at death's door. But more of that shortly.

Jedburgh played host to Bonnie Prince Charlie on 6 and 7 November 1745, during his triumphant march south. The house in which he stayed can still be seen and is easily spotted by the large plaque on the wall that says — more or less — 'Bonnie Prince Charlie Slept Here'. Near to the abbey is the entrance to the Bridewell Jail, part of a building that now houses the Sheriff Court, and further up the High Street is Jedburgh Castle. The original castle was destroyed in 1409 and the present building was for some time the county jail but is now a museum outlining the rigours of 'Jeddart Justice'. This was a system of law by the rope and axe — and when that proved too expensive, rogue Borderers were drowned.

The abbey was founded in 1138 and in the following century formed part of the front line against English intrusion. However, there had been an earlier church on the site and it was here, the story goes, that Northumbrian noble Eadwuld Rus fled after assassinating a Durham bishop. Unfortunately for Rus, sanctuary here did not prove to be all he expected. He was subsequently murdered by a local woman. His body was later dug up and thrown out of the church by a Durham clergyman who was still smarting over the murder of his bishop.

Alexander III was married in the abbey in 1285 — and there is a strange tale that reads like a scene from the *Masque of the Red Death*. It was while the wedding festivities were at their height that a tall, spectral figure with the face of a mouldering corpse appeared to float among them. The wedding guests shrank from the apparition as it glided towards the king and queen. Finally, the guards regained their courage and threw themselves at the figure only to find the winding sheet and mask were empty.

Shortly after this Thomas the Rhymer, a local seer and mystic, announced that on 16 March the following year the country would witness the stormiest day it had ever seen. On that day, Alexander III died in Fife after being thrown from his horse (see Rebel March) – leaving the country without a king and causing civil war between the claimants to the throne and by extension war with England. 'That was the storm I meant,' said Thomas, 'and there was never a tempest which will bring more ill luck to Scotland.'

Those consequent wars have left their scars on the abbey and have wiped the old castle, home of many a Scots king, off the face of the earth. But the English found it hard going against the Jeddart men with their fearsome axes and long pikes. Every time they burned the town the hardy Borderers rebuilt it again. Surrey once wrote to Henry VII during the Rough Wooing: 'I fownd the Scottis at this tyme the boldest men and the hottest I ever sawe. Could 40,000 such men be assembled it would be a dreadful enterprise to withstand them…'

On 23 September 1523, the people of Jedburgh inflicted such terror on Surrey's men that they even began shooting their own horses. Hundreds of the English mounts were stampeded through the burning town – some say by local women – and the English troops, believing this was a daring night attack by rampaging Scots, fired off their arrows and blasted with their hackbutts, killing the terrified beasts.

What the English had started, the Reformation completed and the abbey, like its sister buildings in the Borders, was soon little more than an attractive pile of ruins, its stones lifted to become parts of other buildings.

Mary Queen of Scots came to the town in October 1566 to preside over a circuit court. It was while she was here that she learned that James Hepburn, Earl of Bothwell, had been badly wounded during a disagreement with a notorious Borders freebooter and had been carried to his lair at Hermitage to recuperate. Mary completed her business at Jedburgh pronto and galloped off across the wild moors to pay her lover a visit. She completed the 50-mile round trip in one day,

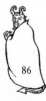

DEVIL'S GALLOP

falling into a bog on the way back and contracting pneumonia. The Queen was desperately ill during the following few days and at one point it was believed she was not long for this world. However a French doctor managed to pull her back from the brink, although in later years while suffering imprisonment in England, she would tell supporters, 'Would God that I had died in Jedburgh.' The house in which she stayed is now a museum.

I left Jedburgh following signs for Newcastle but turned right at a sign for Bonchester Bridge (the B6357). Once there, I turned left, following signs for Newcastleton.

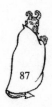

SIXTEEN
Castle Doom

After some time I spotted signs for Hermitage Castle (although this being Scotland that soon stopped). The road here is pretty much part of the farmland and sheep have a propensity for wandering across it, treating motorists with an alarming disdain. These roads, with their attractive hump-backed bridges, always make me feel guilty about driving a car. I feel I should really be in a horse-drawn cart, which strikes me as being a much more civilised mode of travel – the only emissions being natural and good for the roses.

My route took me onto a small side road to the right, signposted 'Steel Road'. This was a very narrow single-track eventually leading to the B6399 where I turned right. Just before another of those quaint bridges, I made a sharp left onto another single-track road. Then, as I came around a bend, I had my first glimpse of Hermitage Castle, dark and gloomy against the surrounding moorland. The building seems to grow directly from the harsh land around it and they say the walls have sunk partly into the earth, weighed down by the burden of centuries of evil.

Hermitage takes its name from the abode of an old monk who lived here before the castle was built to guard what has been described as the bloodiest valley in Britain. The present structure was begun in the fourteenth century, although there had been an earlier wooden one on the site. This earlier castle – a 'motte-and-bailey' (that famous medieval double act) – was built by Sir Nicholas de Soules, who was one of the claimants to the Scottish throne after the death of Alexander III. But it was his son William who helped create the castle's dark reputation.

William was known as 'Bad Lord Soules', for according to legend he was a practitioner of the black arts, reputedly having been initiated by the notorious necromancer Michael Scot (more on him later).

DEVIL'S GALLOP

Soules was a cruel master and a murderous one. He dealt with his tenants as he did his enemies: swiftly and violently. According to local myth, he used local peasants as two-legged oxen, boring holes into their shoulders before yoking them to carts to convey him around his lands. His best pal was said to be Redcap, a particularly fearsome demon with a penchant for attacking travellers at night. He played with his victims like a cat before killing them, catching their blood in his hat (presumably because he liked the sensation of other people's blood going to his head). He was described as being a somewhat grotesque individual with long, prominent teeth and sharp talons for hands. However would-be victims could ward him off by invoking Christ's name, at the sound of which he would dart off like a firework, always leaving behind one of his teeth. No one was ever tempted to place one under their pillow to see what the fairies brought them.

The 'Cout of Kielder' was a giant of a man who lived across the border (there is still an area in Northumberland called Kielder) and he and Bad Lord Soules were mortal enemies. Once, Soules invited him to Hermitage for dinner, apparently to patch things up. The Cout's wife begged her husband not to go, for she believed the Scottish noble was not quite the sort of man to invite neighbours round to try out his new fondue set. But the Cout believed his magical suit of armour (which meant no weapon could kill him) would be enough to protect him.

But when Soules said he wanted to bury the hatchet, he meant it literally. He did not even wait for the pudding to be served before he turned nasty, and he gave his men a sign to attack the guests. Most of them were killed at the table, but the giant Cout was too fast. Running along the tables he fought his way out of the room. Once outside he tried to leap across Hermitage Water, which helped form part of the moat around the castle, but tumbled into the deepest part. At this moment a pair of water wings would have been preferable to his chain mail, for he drowned. (Mind you, he wasn't exactly assisted by Soules and his men, who helpfully pushed him under with spears.)

The Cout's body was buried near the chapel, where the grave is marked by two stones – one at his head and one at his feet.

The murder proved to be the last straw for the people of Liddesdale. They approached King Robert the Bruce and asked him for advice. It was not the first time the King had heard complaints about this border baron and as he had his own problems with the English he told them, 'Hang him, boil him, do anything you like with him but for heaven's sake let me hear no more about him.'

Before he could change his mind, the people converged on Hermitage like extras in some Universal Pictures Frankenstein movie – all mumbled curses and flaming torches. They invited Soules, with the help of clubs, swords and chains, to the old stone circle at Nine Stane Rig near the castle. Once there, Thomas the Rhymer (also known as Thomas of Ercildoune) bound him magically in ropes of sand and Soules was pitched into a boiling cauldron of molten lead. That was the end of the evil Lord of Hermitage, while Redcap sloped off to bleed more people dry. (Perhaps by becoming a soft drinks vendor in London's Hyde Park.)

It is a good grisly story with the villain receiving an end both painful and poetic. The fact that William de Soules *actually* died in a dank, dark and dingy dungeon on Dumbarton Rock, after plotting to remove the crown from Bruce's head and place it on his own, is neither here nor there. His lands came into the possession of the Douglas clan, who perpetrated new horrors at Hermitage. Eighteen years after the death of Bad Lord Soules, Sir William Douglas, irked that he had not been made sheriff of the area, imprisoned Sir Alexander Ramsay – who had been made sheriff – and starved him to death in the castle's prison. Sir William was later murdered in the Ettrick Forest by his godson.

Eventually the castle came into the possession of the Bothwells. It was here that James Hepburn, Mary Queen of Scots's fancy bit, was brought after his fateful fight with Little Jock Elliot. Bothwell had made capturing Elliots one of his missions in life – along with helping to plot the murder of Mary's husband Darnley and getting Mary herself into bed. He set out to snare the famed reiver and threw down the gauntlet of man-to-man combat.

But Bothwell didn't play fair, dropping Elliot from the saddle with a well-aimed pistol shot before moving in closer to finish him off. But as he leaned over his victim, Jock leaped up and plunged his dagger into the Earl three times before finally giving up the ghost. Bothwell was taken back to Hermitage to recuperate, prompting Mary to make her mercy dash and tumble into a marsh on her way.

DEVIL'S GALLOP

Hermitage has a prison tower, furnished only with a small toilet and an even smaller window. When thrown in here for whatever reason – non-payment of rents, reiving or the playing of Celine Dion records – you would find yourself with no light to speak of and no fresh water. However, you did have all the cockroaches you could kill. Meanwhile, above you were two floors of private rooms reserved for more noble prisoners. They had heat, they had light and they had food that didn't wriggle about in their mouth.

And with that charming thought I left the dark delights of Hermitage Castle behind to set off once again cross-country.

SEVENTEEN

Onward Christian Soldiers

Keeping to the small country road that runs alongside Hermitage, passing hills with names such as 'Din Fell', 'Pike Fell', 'Watch Hill' and 'Geordie's Hill', I began to feel as if I was part of the landscape and not merely driving through it. However, the problem with these small roads is that you can meet anything on them, from large American Cadillacs to British four-wheel drives that refuse to make way. On this occasion I encountered a flock of sheep being pushed along by the ubiquitous black-and-white dog and farmer in a car. It was fascinating watching the dog first herding the sheep then, when he fell behind, herding the car as well.

Once past the flock and its hard-working canine, the road took me into a treeless valley filled with dry-stane dykes and even more sheep. At the end of the glen I reached another junction with the A7 and turned right towards Hawick, arriving at Teviothead. I took a left here for Caerlanrig and was soon pulling up at a kirkyard that lies on both sides of the road. Here I found the memorial to Johnny Armstrong, whose family was among the most notorious of the moss troopers of the West and Middle March.

Johnnie Armstrong, or 'Black Jock, Laird of Gilnockie', was one of the most colourful of the Scottish reivers and his arrogance (not to mention his dress sense) soon had James V's nose out of joint. The 17-year-old King was, at the time, trying to bring some order to the lawless border marches and was receiving countless complaints from England about Armstrong's behaviour, for it is said that Johnnie preyed only on those south of the border. So the King wrote a long letter to Black Jock inviting him to Caerlanrig for a powwow under flag of truce. In June 1530, James turned up with 10,000 men at his back while Jock had only 40 or 50. Armstrong was expecting no trouble. However, he was soon to learn not to put his trust in princes, for James swiftly turned on him. Armstrong claimed he was a true Scot but the King was having none of it – and anyway, he didn't much like Johnnie's gold-lined clothes and hat, worth three hundred pounds. Dishing out some Jeddart Justice of his own, James had the border laird and his men hanged from nearby trees. Johnnie Armstrong's name lived on in ballad and legend. In the churchyard there is a stone tablet outlining the story and across the road is the place where Johnnie and his men were reputed to have been buried – marked by a single moss-covered stone.

Returning to the A7 and heading once more towards Hawick, the landscape became richer, losing the blasted feel of the Liddesdale valleys. Here there are real hardwood, broad-leaved trees, not merely the ever-present conifers.

Soon I was in Hawick, which like other towns in the area suffered at the hands of the Scots as well as the English. It was here that many feuding Borderers were brought for summary justice by the axe, the rope and – when cash was tight – by drowning in the Teviot. On one momentous occasion over 20 freebooters were forced to dip more than a big toe into the icy waters. Here also is Drumlanrig Tower – 'The Black Tower' – once one of the most notorious strongholds in the area. It is now a museum tracing the building's story from its beginning in the sixteenth century, through its Douglas-held heyday up until it became part of a hotel in which the likes of Sir Walter Scott and William Wordsworth stayed. The Black Tower was the only building in the town to survive the visit of an English army in 1570, although the present elegant building has long superseded it.

Next on to Selkirk, which nestles among rolling hills of agricultural land. Here I visited the courtroom of Sir Walter Scott, who did much to preserve, develop and create the myths not only of his beloved borderlands but also the rest of Scotland. Unfortunately, it was also largely thanks to him and like-minded Scots that we have the 'tartan-and-shortbread' image of Scotland, that includes the modern-day kilt that is such a travesty of the garb of the real-life Highlanders. Queen Victoria and Prince Albert made all things Scottish stylish in the nineteenth century but it was a false image that ultimately led to such horrors as 'The White Heather Club' and accordion bands. Sir Walter was sheriff of Selkirkshire from 1803 to 1832 and his courtroom is now a museum dedicated to him (complete with a copy of his death mask) and also his friendship with local lad and African explorer Mungo Park.

Also in Selkirk, beside the Victoria Hall, is a monument to the Battle of Flodden where the flower of Scotland withered and died on a bloody field just over the border near Coldstream. Seventy men from Selkirk joined James IV on his ill-fated sortie against the English on 9 September 1513. Only one local man returned from the bloodbath, telling how the Scots and English fought until it became so dark that they could not see who they were striking and the mud beneath their feet turned blood-red. James had led a force of between 60,000 and 100,000 into England that day – 10,000 perished on the rain-soaked field, including the King. His body was found later among the dead and taken to Berwick, where it was embalmed and then sent on to London in a lead casket. It was placed in a monastery but subsequently lost until Elizabethan workmen found it and cut off the head for use as a football. After further adventures (including being put on display) an English noble buried the head in an unmarked grave.

Although Borderers took part in what was up until then Scotland's most disastrous military defeat, others held back from the fray. Lord Hume's forces followed their leader's policy of looking after number one. Later, when the hostilities were over, they looted the corpses of both sides. There was even a suggestion that Hume killed the king and for this reason (amongst others) he and his brother were later executed. This in turn led to his family removing the head of Anthony Darcy, the March Warden whose ambitions and politicking they believed were partly responsible for their Lord's death on the block.

Selkirk is also said to be the site of the church where Sir William Wallace was made Guardian of Scotland. The ruins of the small Kirk o' the Forest are just a few yards from the town centre and there is a plaque claiming the honour for the town. Naturally, there is nothing concrete to support the claim (Carluke in Lanarkshire also claims the honour) but it's as good a place as any.

Just a little way out of Selkirk is the Philiphaugh estate. It was near the bridge across the Yarrow on the A708 (where there are now sports fields) that, on 13 September 1645, a Covenanting army led by Sir George Leslie came upon the much-depleted royalist force led by the Marquis of Montrose. It was to bring to an end the brave Marquis's 'Year of Miracles', during which he had led the bible-thumping enemy a merry dance around Scotland, defeating them whenever they clashed. On this occasion it was the royalists who were defeated, and Montrose was dragged away by his friends. And then, under orders from the ever-present ministers, the Covenanters committed atrocity after atrocity. The remaining royalist forces surrendered and were marched off to Newark Castle (on the A708 heading west) where they were placed in batches against the barmkin wall and shot. The bullet marks can still be seen on the ancient stone.

But that was not the worst these good Christians did that day. In the Montrose camp were 200 followers – women, children, cooks, grooms – all non-combatants but many Roman Catholic, and that was crime enough for these soldiers who, spurred on by their religious leaders, fell on them in a frenzy. Pregnant women were killed, their bellies ripped open until, as one observer noted, 'the fruit of their womb – some in the embryo, some perfectly formed, some crouling for life, and some ready for birth, fell down upon the ground, weltering in the gory blood of their mangled mothers'.

Other women and children were drowned to save the cost of bullets and were pushed under the water with lances. A few who escaped were caught by local people and delivered to Linlithgow where they were also drowned.

Finally the soldiers turned to the black-clad clergy watching the slaughter and cried, 'Have you not yet had your fill of blood?' But the sharp-faced Presbyterians rejoiced, for they were doing God's work, so they believed. It has been argued that the depravity shown here was aggravated by the actions of Montrose's men during the sack of Aberdeen (see Rebel March). But although the Highlanders did commit atrocities (which Montrose deeply regretted) they had been much exaggerated by Covenanter spin-doctors of the day and in no way excuse the despicable bloodlust shown here at Philiphaugh.

I moved on from these green fields that hide such dark memories, and I followed the B6360 from Selkirk to Melrose.

EIGHTEEN
Vampire Slayers

Melrose is dominated by the three-pointed Eildon Hills, which the Romans called Trimontium (and if you can't work out the derivation of that name you should punish yourself by buying another copy of this book).

However, according to legend, there was once a single peak that was split into three when wizard Michael Scot (told you we'd get back to him) challenged one of his pet demons. (He had three such buddies, named Prig, Prim and Pricker.)

Scot himself may have been born here in the Borders. (Or in Fife. Or on a desert island after a Dumbarton merchant sailor got to play the music of love on a mermaid's scales. Take your pick, for they could all be true for all we know.) The fact is Scot was a very learned man who actively condemned witchcraft, but showed so much knowledge of the 'eye of toad, wing of bat' trade that it was firmly believed he must have practised it. Boccaccio called him 'a grand master of necromancy' while Dante included him in his 'Inferno' as one of the wizards of hell. What didn't help Scot's case was, apparently, the gift of prophecy he displayed while living in Palermo when he accurately predicted the death of Frederick III, the Holy Roman Emperor. The news came as a great surprise to those at Court, who held the fervent belief that Freddie was immortal.

It was in the Eildon Hills that Thomas of Ercildoune (Thomas the Rhymer) first met the Fairy Queen who spirited him away to the netherworld. Thomas was much taken with her beauty (for verily, she was a belter) and talked her into a wee bit of coupling in the long grass. She agreed, even though she knew the act of love would steal her beauty. True enough, after they had done the deed and were lying back smoking a cigarette, her looks wasted and she deteriorated into

DEVIL'S GALLOP

DUNDONALD CASTLE

The place that witnessed the power, the glory and the ultimate folly of the Stewart line.

BELOW: FENWICK CHURCH

The kirkyard here is filled with the memorials and graves of Covenanters. Note the 'jougs' hanging from the wall on the left.

ABOVE LEFT: ST JOHN'S TOWER, AYR
All that remains of a medieval church, this was used by Cromwell's forces as an
armoury. Maggie Osborne is said to have been buried in the yard here.

ABOVE RIGHT: WALLACE/BURNS MEMORIAL, LEGLEN WOOD
Tucked away behind bushes in what remains of the wood that
once sheltered Wallace, this cairn is dedicated to the
warrior and the poet who was so inspired by him.

OPPOSITE PAGE BOTTOM: DUNURE CASTLE
It was in the dark vault here that Gilbert
Kennedy roasted the commendator of
Crossraguel Abbey on a spit in order to coerce a
land agreement out of him.

TOWNHOUSE AT CULROSS
Women suspected of being witches were kept in
the tower here until either set free or executed.

BASS ROCK
The island was used as a Covenanter prison.
Tantallon Castle (in the foreground)
withstood the wrath of James I and IV's
army and its cannons for 20 days.

HERMITAGE CASTLE
It is said the walls are sinking into the earth
under the weight of all the evil committed here.

FAR LEFT: JEDBURGH ABBEY.
A strange apparition disturbed the wedding of Alexander III here.

LEFT: STATUE OF JACKIE CROOKSTON, TRANENT
This local lass is shown beating her drum as she leads the protesters in the 'No
Militia' march in 1797.

DUNOTTAR CASTLE, NEAR STONEHAVEN
Wallace slaughtered a garrison here and Covenanters were later imprisoned inside
in horrendous conditions.

ABOVE: RUTHVEN BARRACKS
Jacobites rallied here after
Culloden – only to be told by
Bonnie Prince Charlie that it was
'every man for himself'.

RIGHT: The memorial to the Battle
of Culloden – where, in 1746, the
Jacobite dream died.

OPPOSITE PAGE TOP: Memorials to
two great Scottish heroes: the
statue of Robert the Bruce on
Stirling Castle esplanade and the
Wallace Monument on Abbey
Craig.

OPPOSITE PAGE BOTTOM: Glencoe –
the glen of weeping.

Braes of Balquidder,
where 12 MacGregors
were executed in reprisal
for a brutal murder

ABOVE LEFT: The site of the gibbet on which James of the Glen was hanged
after being wrongly convicted of the Appin murder.

ABOVE RIGHT: The Fairy Tree at Aberfoyle. Wishes are written on rags here and
hung up on the branches. The spirit of a local minister who betrayed the fairy
folks' secrets is said to be trapped in the tree.

an old hag. She still held the power to command Thomas to do her bidding, however, and took him into Elfland where he remained for seven years until he was allowed to return to the land of mortal men, armed with the ability to say a sooth or two. He achieved great fame as a rhyming Mystic Meg – predicting the death of Alexander III was just one of them – but he still pined for the love of the Fairy Queen (who, by the way, regained her beauty) and his fairy friends. Years later, when a hart and a hind were seen walking together down a village street, Thomas realised this was a call from his love and he walked into the hills, never to be seen again.

The Eildons are also said to be the last resting place of King Arthur and his knights, who – it is said – are sleeping there awaiting the clarion call that Britain is once again in grave danger. You can walk around the Eildon Hills if you have a stout pair of shoes and the energy. I had neither so I just admired them from afar.

It was in Melrose, on the site of the present day Waverley Castle Hotel, that Sir Walter Scott of Buccleuch lost a battle against the forces of Douglas, Earl of Angus, on 25 July 1526, in an attempt to free the young James V, whom Red Douglas had in his keeping in Edinburgh Castle.

The home of that Walter Scott's more famous namesake can be seen near Melrose. Abbotsford was the house he bought and worked so hard to keep. Scott's tomb is in ruined Dryburgh Abbey, not far from here, and across the aisle lies the tomb of Earl Haig.

Like its sister establishments in the Borders, Melrose Abbey has seen many trials and tribulations. It was the first of the four Border abbeys to be built by David I – a man who apparently liked to keep his brickies busy, for he also ordered religious buildings to be erected in 11 other parts of Scotland, including Holyrood and Dunfermline.

Apart from praying and singing hymns, the monks here also took a hand in fighting a vampire who had been feeding off the local populace. This particular pain in the neck had been the chaplain to a local noblewoman but he had given his life over to sin, wickedness and karaoke (okay, I made that last bit up). After his death, his body walked by night, sucking the blood from unwary victims. The townspeople did not know what to do about the problem. *Buffy the Vampire Slayer* had not yet been born. So they turned to the monks who formed a 'Scooby Gang' to tackle the sucker. Naturally, this entailed a great deal of praying and fasting before they caught the vampire and burned it to ashes.

Michael Scot may be buried in the abbey grounds (no one is terribly sure), as is the heart of Robert the Bruce. At least, people think it might be. The Bruce died at Cardross on the north bank of the River Clyde on 7 June 1329. One thing he regretted was never having embarked on a pilgrimage to the Holy Land – he was too busy fighting the English to fight Saracens. His last wish was that his heart be taken from his body and carried to Jerusalem. His old friend Sir James Douglas (the Black Douglas) agreed to make the trip, so the heart was placed in a silver casket and he set out from either Montrose or Berwick. He and his party never reached the Holy Land for they offered their services to the Christian Spanish against the invading Moors. Douglas took part in a battle between Seville and Granada during which, according to legend, he threw the casket at the enemy and cried, 'Go forward, brave heart, for I will follow or die.' Follow he did – and die he did. The casket containing the heart of his old friend and King was found beneath his body. They had been through a lot, the Bruce and Black Douglas, and it is fitting they were together at the final moment. It would have been nice if Douglas's heart had been buried alongside Bruce's but it and his skeleton (the flesh having been boiled off in Spain) were interred in a church in the village of Douglas in Lanarkshire. Bruce's heart was supposedly brought here to Melrose, where it lies under a tasteful marker stone.

And there I ended this tour. Returning to Glasgow via the A7, I stopped a while in Galashiels to admire the war memorial – made up in part by a fine statue of a Border Reiver, steel bonnet, flag and horse glistening in the sun. I then took the A72 via Peebles on to the A721, A73 and finally back onto the M8.

REBEL MARCH

CULROSS – BURNTISLAND –
KINGHORN – ANSTRUTHER –
CRAIL – ST ANDREWS –
DUNDEE – ARBROATH –
MONTROSE – DUNOTTAR
CASTLE – STONEHAVEN –
ABERDEEN – COLLIESTON –
SLAINS CASTLE – HARLAW –
HUNTLY CASTLE – KEITH –
ELGIN – FORRES – AULDEARN
– CULLODEN – INVERNESS –
RUTHVEN BARRACKS –
KILLIECRANKIE – DUNKELD –
PERTH – SHERIFFMUIR –
STIRLING – BANNOCKBURN

NINETEEN
The Village That Time Forgot

The town of Cumbernauld grows organically from the low hills around the A80 as it heads north from Glasgow. Cumbernauld was originally designed, to an extent, to take the overspill from the city, where the old crumbling tenements were being bulldozed to make way for roads and soulless high-rise flats. There had been other exoduses from the city too – towards the new housing estates on the fringes like Easterhouse and Drumchapel, and to East Kilbride, the first of the new towns. For many, these new homes marked the beginning of a new era.

I lived in Cumbernauld for three years during the late '60s when it was very much frontier country – when we moved in, our garden was a mound of earth. The thing about these new towns is the speed at which they grow. I swear you can turn away for a second and when you look back they've built another street. They sprawl across the countryside, eating up green fields and forests, crossing streams and rivers, until everything is covered with neat streets and houses, dual carriageways and roundabouts. When I lived here, the town lay entirely on one side of the A80. Now it has extended on the other side almost as far as Kilsyth (which in my day was so far away it seemed like a foreign country).

There are also cemeteries here now, which is more than former inhabitants of the old village had. During the plague years, they had to apply for permission to establish their own burial ground because the populace was dropping like flies and the survivors were fed up walking to Kirkintilloch to plant them.

All this occurred to me as I passed the town on the first leg of this trip. I left the city via the M8, turning onto the M80 (where the speed limit, unaccountably, is only 50 mph). Taking the Kincardine Bridge turn-off onto the M876, I passed by Falkirk, the site of William Wallace's ignominious defeat on 22 July 1298, when the Scottish barons' betrayal effectively ended his military hopes. Bonnie Prince Charlie had better luck on 17 January 1746 when his Highlanders took on the royal forces near the town.

I crossed Kincardine Bridge, which spans the Forth as it cuts through a flat plain that stretches towards the Ochil Hills. I then took a right turn, following signs to Culross. In this picturesque village I picked up the next instalment in the story of the pregnant Thenew. As you will remember, the young lady had been cast adrift by her dad, Loth, after he found out she was 'in the family way'. Eventually, the tides brought her to Culross, where the shadowy St Serf had a mission (although some accounts claim that St Serf was not active until 200 years later). Here she gave birth to the child on the shore and named him Kentigern. The boy was taken under the wing of the kindly old priest and soon became known as 'Munghu', which means 'Dear One'. It was no surprise that the young lad would eventually take up a missionary position, as it were, for he soon displayed a tendency towards the miraculous. One day, young thugs killed the old priest's pet robin and Kentigern brought it back to life. A robin forms part of the Glasgow coat of arms, as Kentigern (or Mungo) would later form a monastery on a point above the Molendinar Burn, near the Clyde, which would mark the beginning of the city. His connection with Culross is marked by a ruined chapel said to be built on the site of his birth to the north-east.

But Culross is worth visiting for more than St Mungo's early life. The village is National Trust property and as such the houses are very much as they would have been three centuries ago. There is a palace here, once owned by descendants of Robert the Bruce. Sir George Bruce also owned both the salt pans and coal-mines that helped the area prosper. In 1617, King James I (VI of Scotland) came back for a brief visit to his homeland and particularly wanted to visit the Culross mine. Sir George took him down into the maze of tunnels, eventually emerging on an island on the middle of the river. James, being James, panicked, believing this was some sort of assassination plot. But he calmed down when it was explained to him that a boat was moored nearby to take him the mile back to shore, where a magnificent banquet awaited him in the palace.

Culross did not escape the mass lunacy of the witch hunts. The Town House was built in 1626 and witches were imprisoned in its tower until either set free or (more often than not) executed. One such witch somehow left a footprint here on a stone stairway on her way to the stake. Another was placed in stocks in her cell while her jailers warmed themselves in front of a fire in another room. They heard a scream and found the woman on the cobbled street below, her legs broken. The Devil had released her from the stocks, it was believed, and was flying away with her when the witch took fright and slipped from his grasp. It took four men to carry her to the stake.

Leaving Culross with its charming narrow cobbled streets and brightly coloured red-roofed houses, I took the coast road (the B9037) passing through the small town of Torryburn, until I reached the junction with the A985. I followed this until it passed underneath the Forth Road Bridge and became the A921 – the Fife Coastal Route.

DEVIL'S GALLOP

TWENTY
Kings, Queens and Knaves

As I travelled through Aberdour towards Burntisland and Kinghorn I was treated to superb views across the Forth towards Edinburgh, where I easily spotted the landmarks of Arthur's Seat and the Castle.

In Burntisland is Rossend Castle, where a young French poet, Pierre de Chatelard once made something of a nuisance of himself. The beauty of Mary Queen of Scots had so mightily transfixed him that he began to stalk her. This came to a head when he was discovered in her bedroom and was subsequently instructed to quit the Court. But his poet's temperament would not allow him to forsake his true-love, so he followed the Queen when she toured Fife in 1563 and at Rossend he once again hid in her bedchamber, catching the Queen while she was climbing into her jammies. The sight of the bare royal flesh was too much for Pierre and he forced his attentions on her. As he was not of royal blood, and was unlikely to help Mary keep her own throne *or* lead her onto the English one, she screamed for help. The poet was caught, taken to St Andrews and executed in the market place. Mary watched the whole thing, although to be fair she may have been forced to do so by her half-brother, James Stewart, Lord Moray. Rossend Castle is now used as offices by a firm of architects, its gardens covered by houses and a children's playground.

A short distance from Burntisland, at Kinghorn, a tall stone cross stretches into the sky from the roadside. This memorial marks the spot where Alexander III was found dead, an event that led in turn to the rise and fall of William Wallace, the bloody Wars of Independence and the emergence of Robert the Bruce as a national hero.

Alexander came to the throne in 1249 when he was just eight years of age. In his time he did much for his country – notably defeating the

Vikings at Largs in 1263. He also formed an alliance with the English (albeit an uneasy one) by marrying Longshanks's sister, Margaret. She gave him two sons and a daughter but Alexander outlived all of them. Then in 1285 he married Yolande, the daughter of a powerful French noble. On 18 March 1286, Alexander left Edinburgh to rejoin his young wife at Kinghorn Castle (of which nothing now remains). The weather was filthy and the ferrymen had to be bribed to take the King across the choppy waters of the Forth. Once safely on the other side the King dashed ahead, no doubt eager to reach his beloved Yolande and get down to the business of providing the nation with a male heir. But on the cliffs above this spot his horse stumbled and the King was thrown from the saddle to his death on the shore below.

Leaving the memorial behind, I continued along the coastal route, passing Kirkcaldy, and Ravenscraig Castle (one of the first in the country built with artillery in mind) through Dysart (where the tollbooth served as a powder magazine during the wars with Cromwell) and onto the A955. I passed a sign for West Wemyss where, in February 1564, Mary Queen of Scots first met Henry Stuart (Lord Darnley) in a castle perched on a cliff over the rocky beach. The 19-year-old youth was Queen Elizabeth's favoured marriage partner for her Scottish cousin, but the scheming English monarch had let it be known officially that she was against the match. This feigned resistance to Darnley only served to stimulate Mary's interest in him. The young man was also, on the surface at least, quite a catch. He had charm, wit and good looks. Unfortunately, he also had ambition. He knew that if he could win Mary over, he would be in prime position to make himself King of Scotland. As usual, Mary let her heart rule her head and she allowed herself to be won over by this primping, preening puppy – leading to the murders of Rizzio (and Darnley himself) and ultimately the loss of her throne.

Pressing ahead on the A955 past Buckhaven and Methil, I finally came back to the A915. Rising in the distance was Largo Law, a hill with links to the wizard Michael Scot. He had ordered his three familiars (you will remember they were called Prig, Prim and Pricker) to level this hill but they had only thrown one shovelful off before they were called away on other demonic business. That shovelful – now called Norrie's Law – can be seen to the side of the hill today.

Lower Largo was the home of Alexander Selkirk, the real-life castaway whose life on a desert island inspired Daniel Defoe to write *Robinson Crusoe*. Upper Largo was the home of another seafarer, Sir Andrew Wood, who was admiral of what the Scots amusingly called a navy. In 1481, with only two ships, he forced English convoys out of the Forth and the Clyde – and in later years continued to make sailors from south of the border decidedly seasick. A canal linked his house to the old church to allow him to sail to services in style.

From Upper Largo I followed the signs for Anstruther, and turned onto the A917. This is one of those attractive villages that pepper the east coast, and its past as a mainstay of the fishing and whaling industries forms much of its attraction to tourists today. Its fisheries museum boasts a reconstruction of a fisherman's cottage and an arch made from the jawbone of the largest whale ever caught in the Arctic. The town gave the world many great sailors, including John Anstruther who turned privateer to help the army of the Marquis of Montrose in his war against Cromwell and the Covenanters. But it was stories of English pirates that drew me here – attempts by local men to bring them to justice almost kicked off an international incident.

In 1586 some Suffolk buccaneers were making pests of themselves all along the east coast. On one occasion they hijacked a barque on its way into Anstruther and killed a crew member. They also raided another ship near Pittenweem before sailing home with their booty. But they did not get away Scot-free, for some Anstruther fishermen were in hot pursuit. They were joined in the chase by a Scottish war vessel and sailed all the way to Suffolk, where they brought the pirates to heel, capturing six of their number. The English authorities were, naturally, none too pleased with this mini-invasion. The fact that the Scottish warship had been forcing English shipping along the way to pay homage to Scotland did not help. When the facts were fully explained, English judges allowed the captured buccaneers to be taken away. Four were sent to St Andrews to be hanged, while the remaining two were brought to Anstruther where they danced the hangman's jig at the end of the esplanade, near the church.

Crail is another cute fishing village, but one which has had the temerity to anger the Devil. The parishioners had decided it was time they had a new church and so they started to build one at the eastern end of the spacious market place. Auld Nick, who was holidaying on the Isle of May on the Firth of Forth (Ibiza being full) took exception to this and tried to demolish the building by hurling a huge rock at it. He almost made it too – for although the boulder split in mid-air, one part landed very close to the church gates where it can still be seen, complete with the mark of the Devil's thumb. Locals used to sharpen their spears and arrows on the stone, believing it brought them good luck. The other half of the stone, by the way, landed to the north, on the beach at Balcomie.

Further along the A917 I reached St Andrews – a town that may have had its roots in the arrival of the bones of a saint but that history has subsequently proved far from saintly.

DEVIL'S GALLOP

TWENTY-ONE
Cross Road

It was during the fourth century that Regulus, or St Rule, first came to these shores accompanied by eight hermits, three virgins, two deacons and a priest. He had set sail from Patras, in Greece, a considerable time earlier, having been told in a dream to travel far to the west where God would give him some sort of sign. He took with him what might today seem like a curious cargo: basically a casket containing a bone from an arm, three fingers of a right hand, a tooth and a kneecap. These were all genuine, authenticated, bona fide relics of St Andrew, who had been martyred in Patras on a X-shaped cross. Eventually God did come up with a sign – a fierce storm that wrecked the ship and cast its passengers onto a bay in the East Neuk of Fife, where the local Pictish king met them on the beach.

'We come in peace,' said St Rule, in his own language, holding up St Andrew's bones before adding, 'He comes in pieces.'

The King looked at his own holy man and asked, in Pictish, 'What did he say?'

'Don't know,' said the advisor, 'It's all Greek to me. Let's kill them.'

'Sounds good to me,' replied the King, no doubt eyeing the virgins and planning to remedy that condition as soon as possible. But before his men could heft their first spear, a white 'X' appeared in the blue sky. The King took this as a sign from heaven and decided it was a good time to turn Christian. And that was how Scotland took the white cross on the blue background as its flag – at least according to Fifers, who snort in derision at the Athelstaneford story (see Border Raid).

St Rule settled here, making St Andrews a centre of religious life in Scotland. In 1411 it would become the first Scottish town to have its own university. It also boasts the oldest golf club in the world, making it the official home of the game. In 1457, golf was becoming too popular and the authorities were concerned that people were ignoring archery which, let's face it, is handier in time of war than a knack for putting. So the Scottish Parliament decreed that 'futeball and golfe be utterly cryit doun'. But 100 years later, the Archbishop of St Andrews declared that every citizen had the right to tee off on the town's links. They could also shoot, play 'futeball' and cut up the links if they wanted to. Fifty years later, however, at the end of the sixteenth century, the church was less enamoured with the game, for parishioners were thinking more about holes in one than Holy Ones, so fines were introduced as punishment to anyone who missed services.

But the Church – both Catholic and Protestant – had more to worry them here than golf. Over 800 years ago, when they decided to build St Rule's tower, it is said a giant tried to knock it down with a huge boulder. The cathedral itself was begun in 1160 and took 150 years to complete. Then, in 1304, along came Edward Longshanks to steal the lead from the roof when the local bobby wasn't looking. A fire all but destroyed the place later that century, with wind and weather causing further damage. Later, Knox's reformers 'reformed' the stonework into rubble and in 1649 the town used the huge stones to protect itself against Cromwell's troops. The cannibalisation of the material continued from then on, as locals picked up whatever they needed to build their own homes, byres and pavements from the old cathedral.

Even prior to the ravages of war, weather and wreckers, the cathedral was often not treated with the respect it deserved. Robert the Bruce apparently once rode his horse down the central aisle, while in the early fifteenth century Canon Thomas Plater stabbed Prior Robert of Montrose to death here. The prior was buried in state but the canon was entombed in a dunghill.

Religious leaders tried to keep a lid on unrest by burning whoever took their fancy. Paul Crawar, a doctor from Bohemia, was executed in 1432 under orders of James I who did not like him preaching free love and an early form of socialism, among other things. He was burned at the stake in the market place, a brass ball wedged into his mouth to prevent him from spouting any more hair-brained ideas. An 'X' marks the spot on the cobbles.

DEVIL'S GALLOP

By the reign of James V, Protestantism was making its mark and the Roman Catholic hierarchy was getting worried. Patrick Hamilton was a great-grandson of James II, although his side of the family was stained with illegitimacy. He studied under Luther himself in Wittenberg and was sent back to Scotland to do what he could to further the cause of the Reformation. He brought with him a Lutheran Bible, and some fiery words. The young preacher was an immediate hit – too big a hit, in fact, for the authorities. In 1528 they had him arrested and sentenced to be burned in front of the university. On 29 February he was tied to the stake surrounded by faggots, but they failed to kindle properly and so some gunpowder was thrown on to speed things along. The resulting explosion merely injured Hamilton's left hand. No great conflagration entertained the congregation that day and Hamilton ultimately suffered six excruciatingly painful hours before finally dying. While he slowly roasted, the crowd urged him to convert back to Catholicism but he told them, 'You are late with your advice. If I had chosen to recant I would not be here.'

A bale of hay was thrown onto the fire but this only caused a jet of flame to reach out and burn a monk's cowl, which served him right. When a spectator asked Hamilton for a sign that he still clung to his beliefs, he raised three fingers of his injured hand, to symbolise the Holy Trinity, and held them there until he gave up the Holy Ghost. (A symbolic two-finger salute would have been more defiant, I think.) His initials were laid in the cobblestones on the site of the pyre, outside the entrance to St Salvator's College.

Patrick Hamilton's death was designed to make people think twice about embracing the new religion, but it had the opposite effect. As one noble said to the Bishop of St Andrews afterwards, 'If ye burn any mair, let them be burned in the cellar for the reek o' Patrick Hamilton has affected as many as it blew upon.'

George Wishart, a former student of St Andrews, also began to preach the doctrine of reform. He had been sent to Scotland by Henry VIII to help speed up the process of marrying off the young Mary to his son Edward. But Wishart's preaching angered the Scottish authorities – and Cardinal David Beaton in particular, who opposed any idea of such a marriage. In 1546 Wishart was implicated in a plot to assassinate Beaton. When they came to arrest him, his bodyguard John Knox was ready to make a fight of it but Wishart, who appeared to be looking forward to a spot of martyrdom, said, 'Return to your bairns and God bless you. One is enough for sacrifice.'

The subsequent trial was swift and Wishart was burned at the stake, although unlike Hamilton they showed some mercy by strangling him first. Cardinal Beaton, a cruel and vicious man, was unmoved by the spectacle. But he was also unaware that this death would light a fire that would never be extinguished – and that would soon scorch even him. For the torch of reform had now passed to Knox and similar minded men – and peaceful martyrdom was not their idea of setting the world aflame. George Wishart's initials in the cobblestones below the windows of Beaton's palace mark the site of his pyre.

Beaton's palace apartments formed part of St Andrews Castle, which perches on the coastline above the beach. In May 1546, three months after Wishart's death, three men entered the castle pretending to be part of the small army of masons and labourers who were re-fortifying it against any future attack by Henry's forces. Later more men arrived at the gate and demanded to see the Cardinal who, having spent the night with his mistress, was at the time sleeping the sleep, if not of the just, then certainly of the just after. More armed men arrived and the gatekeeper was killed, his body tossed into the moat. With the aid of the three men already inside, the invaders stormed Beaton's room. They wanted him to show some remorse for the execution of George Wishart but the petulant prelate merely ordered them to leave him alone because he was a priest – probably not the wisest thing to say under the circumstances. The angry men killed him on the spot, then draped his body over the battlements by an arm and a leg to advertise their deed. John Knox said the murder was 'a godly act', justifying it by suggesting that Beaton was not only the lover of Queen Mary of Guise but also that he had conspired with her to poison King James V following the rout at Solway Moss.

Beaton's body was dumped in the castle's infamous 'bottle' dungeon, and salted, said Knox, 'to keep it from stinking'. This dungeon is so-called because, believe it or not, it is shaped like a bottle. Hewn out of solid rock, this horrendous pit is 24 feet deep and 15 feet wide.

With the castle now in the hands of the Protestants, Henry VIII showed his support by sending provisions, cash and many good wishes – but no troops. The Earl of Arran (then Regent) rolled up with siege engines and began to tunnel from the other side of what is now the roadway almost to the base of the front tower. The Protestants heard of this and, humming 'Anything You Can Do', dug their own tunnel to intercept Arran's human moles. Their plan thus scuppered, the besiegers retreated, although their mine and the defenders' counter-mine can still be viewed today – one of the most unusual attractions of any Scottish castle.

A year on, Mary of Guise arrived with a French fleet, the Protestants soon realised that all was lost, and surrendered. Knox and his fellow leaders were arrested but mercy was shown, and they were sentenced to 19 months in the French galleys. But this was not the last Scotland would hear of John Knox.

I left St Andrews and headed inland, in search of the scene of another bloody murder. Once again the victim was a St Andrews archbishop. Maybe those guys should've been paid danger money.

TWENTY-TWO

The City of Discovery

Archbishop James Sharp was not a popular man. He had been a minister in Crail before setting off in 1660 to plead the cause of the Presbyterian Church. But a year later he switched vestments and was ordained as an Episcopal archbishop and sent back to Scotland to hound Covenanters. After Rullion Green, he demanded that Covenanter prisoners be executed, even going to the lengths of delaying papers from the king asking for mercy. (At least, that's what the Covenanters said later.)

Finally, a band of nine Covenanters decided to do something about him. It was 3 May 1679 and Sharp was returning to St Andrews from Edinburgh across Magus Muir, accompanied by some servants and his daughter. The gang stopped the coach and the Archbishop was dragged out, pleading for his life and offering them cash. One of the men, David Hackston, declined to take part in what was turning into a very ugly affair and rode off. The others cut Sharp to pieces in front of his horrified daughter.

Although the authorities launched a manhunt to bring the 'assassinates' to justice, it would be some years before any of them was punished. Although Hackston took no part in the actual murder, he was hanged after being captured during the Battle of Aird's Moss in Ayrshire. Another of the gang died at the Battle of Bothwell Bridge. Yet another was actually arrested for not attending services and refusing to toast the king but during his imprisonment let it slip that he had been on the muir that dark night. He dangled on a rope in Edinburgh before his head and hands were cut off. His torso was displayed at the site of the murder for ten months before being buried.

To reach the site of the Archbishop's death, I took the B939 road from St Andrews, following signposts for Cupar. About four miles out,

I reached a crossroads where a sign for the Peat Inn pointed left. Soon after, a signpost indicated a shady parking place on the right. I parked here and followed the path through the woods, not at all sure I was on the right track, until I reached the pyramid shaped memorial. (Also not far from here, in a small enclosure in a field, there is an unrelated Covenanters memorial. This marks the spot where five of these God's Soldiers were executed after being captured at Bothwell Bridge.)

To reach the A917 again, I retraced my steps to the crossroads but continued straight over, following the road for Guardbridge until I reached the junction with the coast road. I then turned left towards the Tay Road Bridge and Dundee.

The road bridge is, of course, comparatively modern. It was built in 1966 but the nearby rail bridge is older (built between 1883 and 1887). At two miles wide it is the longest rail bridge in Europe.

The first Tay Rail Bridge opened in June 1878. It had taken seven years to build but would take considerably less time to demolish. On Sunday, 28 December 1879, Scotland was lashed by severe storms. At 7.14 p.m., a train carrying 71 passengers began the crossing from Fife – a journey that should have taken only ten minutes. About halfway across, the bridge collapsed in the strong winds and the train plunged into the foaming waters of the Tay. None of the passengers survived – although a spaniel did apparently swim through the gale to safety.

As I drove across the bridge, I could see that the landscape is dominated by Dundee Law, the huge volcanic rock rising out of the city's heart. There is an iron-age fort on top and the energetic visitor is rewarded with stunning views from its summit. Naturally, I was not feeling that athletic. In Dundee HMS *Unicorn* is also moored. It is the oldest British built ship still afloat and now houses a Royal Navy museum, as well as the *Discovery*; the ship that took Scott on his ill-fated Antarctic expedition.

It was in Dundee that William Wallace allegedly struck another blow against the English. With life getting too hot for him in Ayrshire, according to Blind Harry, his mother brought him to the home of his uncle at Kilspindie, between Dundee and Perth. During this time Wallace attended school in Dundee, learning his three Rs: Reading, Rioting and Roughhousing. One day, Wallace donned his best suit of green and set off to catch the eyes of Dundee lassies near to the (now non-existent) castle. A young Englishman by the name of Selbie made the mistake of asking how a mere Scot could afford such fine togs. He then proceeded to tempt providence by reaching for Wallace's dagger. In a flash, Wallace leaped at the youth, pinned him to the wall and gave him one end of the knife. If he had stabbed him in the head, Selbie would have been a *real* dirk head.

Wallace ran into a nearby inn where the landlady dressed him in women's clothes and placed him at a spinning wheel until the pursuing English had passed. The stone on which he sat is now in the city's McManus Museum. After that, Wallace and his mother trekked overland to Dunfermline and then home (either to Renfrewshire or Ayrshire, depending on your loyalties).

The site of Selbie's murder is commemorated in a plaque in Dundee's High Street, near to the steps leading to St Paul's Cathedral. The plaque makes the following grandiose claim:

Site of Castle of Dundee
Destroyed circa 1314. Near this spot William Wallace struck
the first blow for independence circa 1288

But Wallace was not yet finished with Dundee. In 1297, after having attacked both Dunottar and Aberdeen, he returned here and met Andrew De Moray, a young man from the north with similar views to his on the English. De Moray was also proving most unpopular with Edward Longshanks, and by joining forces the two troublesome young men were ready to take on the English in a fully-fledged battle which came at Stirling Bridge.

Just in front of the small plaque in the High Street is a statue of Admiral Duncan of Camperdown and Dundee, an old sea-dog who hunted for Bonnie Prince Charlie off the west coast of Scotland in those dangerous days after Culloden. He achieved great fame in later years by giving a Dutch fleet a battering in October 1797 off Camperdown.

Further up the High Street – past the site of the old town house in the civic square where public executions used to take place – is the Old Steeple. Dating from 1442, it is the oldest building in Dundee and first felt the heavy hand of warfare in 1548 when the English set fire to it. In 1588 it was used as a prison and then in 1651 came the bloodiest act in its history. Cromwell was at the time trying to pacify Scotland and he sent General Monck to bring Dundee to heel. The town's governor, General Lumsden, took his garrison into the steeple and prepared for siege. For three days the English tried to breach the eight-foot-thick walls but failed. Then they turned to more insidious means – and set alight layers of damp straw around the bottom of the tower. The thick, noxious smoke seeped into the steeple, forcing Lumsden to surrender. The Roundheads summarily executed the 800 men and 200 women and children. The marks from the musket fire can still be seen on the floor of the tower. General Lumsden's head was spiked and put on display on the roof of the steeple.

In 1715, when James Edward Stuart, the Old Pretender, visited the city during the short-lived rising, the bells of this steeple rang with such force that they cracked. It was actually a waste of effort on the part of the bellringers for it wasn't long before he scuttled back to France.

I spent the night in Broughty Ferry nearby, sharing fish and chips with some insistent seagulls on the banks of the Tay as the sun sank magnificently from a patchwork sky of multi-coloured clouds.

This, indeed, was the life.

TWENTY-THREE
Anything to declare

The founding of Arbroath Abbey came about through the disagreements between England's Henry II and his Chancellor, Thomas Beckett, the famously murdered Archbishop of Canterbury. Henry wanted to limit the Church's power and Thomas, naturally, was none too enamoured with the idea. In 1170, four knights, believing they were doing their King a favour, brutally murdered Beckett in Canterbury.

In Scotland, William the Lion was horrified at the news of the death of a man who had been an old friend. He was also unhappy with Henry, who refused to part with lands in England that he insisted belonged to him. In 1175, William sided with Henry's rebellious relatives and went to war. Things came unstuck for the Scottish King at Alnwick in Northumberland when he was captured and treated to some of the English King's hospitality in Normandy.

It was then that William discovered just how, apparently, his battle plans had gone so awry. It was believed Thomas Beckett had aided Henry from beyond the grave. It was said that a barefoot Henry had spent a night kneeling before St Thomas's shrine, his skin itching from a hair shirt, praying, weeping and generally feeling sorry for himself. That following morning he was whipped by 80 of the clergy. At the very moment Henry left Canterbury – no doubt in search of a paracetamol – William of Scots was captured.

William (and Henry) believed that Beckett's spirit had been so moved by the English King's repentance that it helped his army to victory. Greatly impressed by this feat, the Scottish monarch, on his release in 1178, set about founding an abbey in Arbroath dedicated to the murdered Archbishop. The abbey's seal depicts Beckett's martyrdom.

From Broughty Ferry, I took the A92 to Arbroath where I followed the many signposts to the abbey. William the Lion was buried here, although his tomb was lost for many years, thanks to Reformation wrecking-crews and a subsequent collapse of the roof. It was not until 1816, when workmen came to clear up some of the debris, that the tomb was discovered again. Earlier in the twentieth century, the bones were reburied and the simple stone slab we see today was laid over them.

However, patriotic Scots come here to see the place where the most famous document in the country's history was written – the Declaration of Arbroath, Scotland's declaration of independence.

The original letter was a plea to the Pope to use his influence to have the English leave its poorer nation to the north in peace (the historical equivalent of 'telling your big brother'). However, Pope John XX was at that time (April 1320) siding with Edward II against the Scots, primarily because he had excommunicated Bruce and those bishops who supported him.

The letter, perhaps written by the Abbot Bernand De Linton, begins with some quite stupendously obsequious crawling to the Holy Father. It then gets in some subtle barbs at the English King, pointing out that although he was a magnificent guy, he did commit much slaughter, had imprisoned the leaders of the Church, burned and looted religious houses, massacred communities and was generally an absolute rotter. (Of course, the fact that the Scots did their own slaughtering, imprisoning, burning, looting and massacring doesn't get a mention.)

Next along comes reference to 'our most valiant sovereign', Robert the Bruce – and a section that still stirs any Scots heart:

> Yet Robert himself, should he turn aside from the task that he has begun, and yield Scotland or us to the English King and people, we should cast out as the enemy of us all, as subverter of our rights and of his own, and should choose another king to defend our freedom; for as long as a hundred of us are left alive, we will yield in no least way to English dominion. We fight not for glory nor for wealth nor for honours; but only and alone we fight for freedom, which no good man surrenders but with his life.

The Olympic-class crawling seemed to work – for Pope John did indeed drop a few words in Edward's shell-like. But Edward was having none of it. He believed the Scots were helping stir up dissent in England, so he gathered an army that burned and looted as far as Edinburgh before Bruce's scorched earth policy forced it to retreat. Finally, Edward did agree to an uneasy truce and even the Pope recognised Bruce's succession to the Scottish throne. Later, the Pope would even lift the excommunication order, but by then Bruce was dead.

The importance of Arbroath was not lost on the scamps who liberated the Stone of Destiny from Westminster on Christmas Day 1950. Despite a nationwide hunt, the stone – stolen from Scone centuries before by Longshanks – was not found until the following April, when it was left at the abbey for police to find. It was a nice touch but it still took almost 50 years before the stone was officially returned to Scotland.

On leaving Arbroath, the road eventually curved away from the coast to take me across some rich farmland. In the distance the Grampian Mountains rose past the lush, September fields. As the road began again to turn towards the coast, I spotted the ruins of a red castle jutting out above a sandy bay. This was, surprisingly enough, Red Castle, built during the fifteenth century on the site of an earlier fort where William the Lion stayed when checking up on the construction of Arbroath Abbey.

TWENTY-FOUR

Carry on Sieging

On 8 July 1296, Edward Longshanks camped near Montrose with an army of 34,000 men. This was part of his great push north to teach the Scots a lesson in manners, and he eventually reached as far as Elgin. John Balliol had disappointed him by not only refusing to help the English fight the French, but by actually forging an alliance with the hated enemy. Edward, furious that he had misjudged Balliol, decided that what he could not do by subtle means, he would do by the sword. So Berwick (then a Scottish town) was sacked – with a death toll so high the blood flowed in the streets like water. Then he took Dunbar, all but destroying the Scottish army at Spott Burn. The two Kings finally came face-to-face in a small church at Strathcathro, near Brechin. Edward forced Balliol to renounce the treaty with France and also arranged for a most demeaning ceremony in Montrose Castle (of which nothing now remains). Here, Edward took the Scottish Crown from the head of the miserable Balliol and announced he was King no more. To add to his shame, the surcoat bearing the Lion Rampant was unceremoniously ripped from his shoulders and thrown to the floor. From this point on Balliol would be known as 'Toom Tabard', or 'empty coat'. This broken and pitiful man who would be king – but who lacked both the ruthlessness and the blood-lust needed – was imprisoned (in some comfort) in the Tower of London with his son.

Edward then began the great plundering of Scotland's heritage. The Stone of Destiny and the Black Rood of St Margaret (said to be a portion of the True Cross of Christ) were stuffed into Edward's swag bag along with valuable royal documents. On his way back to London, Edward stopped again in Berwick where he accepted the fealty of many Scottish barons and nobles. They added their names to a document with so many dangling seals and ribbons that it became known as the Ragman's Roll. And it is from this that the word 'rigmarole' may be derived.

The following year, Wallace repaid Edward's treatment of Balliol in Montrose by slaughtering the English garrison. Five hundred years later, coins minted during the reign of Edward I were found under the High Street – thought probably to have been left by a dead English soldier.

Water laps on three sides of the town and I reached it by crossing a bridge over the stretch that links Montrose Basin with the sea. Sir James Douglas and his men may have sailed from the old harbour here on their adventurous trip with Bruce's heart towards the Holy Land, and the Old Pretender quietly slipped out of Scotland from the harbour after the debacle of the 1715 uprising. But in between these two embarkations, a group of rowdy Royalists brought death and violence to the narrow streets and quiet gardens of the town.

James Graham, fifth Earl and first Marquis of Montrose had already come out against the Covenanters, if not the National Covenant itself. Montrose did not like the heavy-handed way the Covenanters went about things. When the Solemn League united with Cromwell against the King, he could not bring himself to support them so he offered his services to Charles I. Montrose had now set himself on a path towards glory, betrayal and death.

On 24 April 1644, a group of young Royalist hotheads rode into town intent on seizing its two brass cannons. But the townspeople had been warned of the raid and were ready for them. The fighting spilled over from the city gates into the market place. The Royalists managed to gain possession of the cannons and hauled them to the harbour where they planned to sail to Aberdeen. But again the local people, faithful to the Covenant, were waiting for them and 40 musketeers unleashed a murderous fusillade from a ship. Realising they would never get the artillery out of the town, the Royalist commander had the cannons pushed into the sea before he and his remaining men fought their way to safety.

Two years later, the Marquis was ordered by Charles to disband his army. The King, realising his cause was lost, had surrendered to the Covenanter forces. It was agreed under treaty that the King's man in

Scotland would be allowed to leave the country from Montrose harbour. But, surprisingly for such a busy port, there were no ships at berth during August 1646 – and James Graham had to be out of the country by the 31st. A ship did arrive on the final day but it was a wreck and the drunken master on board boasted that his orders were to hug the coast on the way south to allow English ships to arrest his passenger. Finally, on 3 September, Montrose left Scotland disguised as a servant, on a small boat sailing from Stonehaven. The man who almost won Scotland back for his king was bound for Norway, believing that he would never return to his native soil. But he would be back to fight for his king eventually, only to be betrayed by a Scottish noble for a handful of silver.

I left Montrose, and travelled north until I saw a sign for Dunottar Castle. A short distance further on I had my first glimpse of the castle itself, perched magnificently on a rocky promontory and looking every inch a medieval stronghold. Along with Eilean Donan and Kilchurn, this is arguably one of the most photographed castles in Scotland. As I walked down the path from the small car park on a sunny September afternoon, all I could hear were shutters clicking and cameras whirring. Dunottar's photogenic properties were not lost on director Franco Zefferelli either, who used it as one of the locations for his version of *Hamlet*, starring Mel Gibson.

Dunottar perches on top of a rocky mound 160 feet above the sea with only a thin strip of rock linking it to the mainland. The deep chasm that all but separates it from the land has proved very handy over the centuries, both for keeping people out and keeping them in. When Cromwell's troops besieged the place for eight months in 1652, they were surprised to find that only 35 men had kept them at bay. The defenders had also managed to smuggle out the Crown Jewels of Scotland during the siege.

Charles II had just been crowned at Scone. Naturally, Cromwell, as Lord Protector of the Commonwealth, saw it as a direct challenge to his authority. So Oliver's army marched northwards, intending not only to kill and burn anything that got in their way, but also to seize the royal regalia of crown, mace and sceptre which had been sent to the castle for safekeeping. The English turned up at the castle gates and someone, probably sounding like Sid James, called out to the garrison, 'We've come to get our hands on the King's Regalia!'

'Ooh, matron!' replied a voice from the ramparts, sounding very like Kenneth Williams.

'Let us in,' demanded another Englishman, not impressed with all this carry-on.

'Not by the hairs on our chinny-chin-chins,' came the reply from a Scot who had obviously wandered into the wrong script. Nevertheless, the English huffed and puffed but failed to blow down the walls, which were built to withstand everything but the heaviest of siege engines. However, after a few months the heavy stuff arrived and a few well-placed shots soon had the Scottish forces realising that they were not as secure as they had once thought.

The King's private papers were sewn into a belt worn by Anne Lindsay (a woman related to the wife of the castle's commander George Ogilvy). She sauntered through the English lines unchallenged. Meanwhile, the regalia were lowered on a very long rope from the castle walls where a servant girl was ostensibly out collecting dulse, a form of edible seaweed. The girl hid the crown, mace and sceptre at the bottom of her basket and took them to the parish church at Kinkell where they were hidden under the floor until the Reformation in 1660. The rampaging Roundheads, raging at the removal of the regalia (which is easier to type than say), tortured George Ogilvy and his wife but they insisted the jewels had been shipped abroad. These days, the Crown Jewels can be seen in Edinburgh Castle – although over the centuries there has been some suggestion that some of the gems may have been replaced by 'paste' replicas, for the Stewarts were often in need of quick cash.

Prior to all this – around 1297 – the castle had a visit from William Wallace who trapped the garrison of occupying English troops in the church and burned them alive. Some of the soldiers fell to their deaths while trying to escape by climbing down the steep rock face. You may wonder whether the Scots were conscience stricken over this bloodthirsty deed but Blind Harry claims Wallace put their minds at rest, telling them, 'Thai rewid nocht was in to the toun of Ayr, our trew barrownis quhen that hair hangyt that.' So I hope that clears things up . . .

DEVIL'S GALLOP

In 1645, the Earl Marischal refused to come out to play with Montrose and closed Dunottar's gates against him. In anger, Montrose burned Stonehaven (a few miles north, and my next port of call). From the castle battlements, the Earl sadly watched as the smoke rose from the town, and was comforted by the words of a Covenanter minister, Andrew Cant, who said: 'Trouble not, for the reek will be a sweet smelling savour in the nostrils of the Lord.' This would have come as small consolation to those people watching their no-claims bonus go up in smoke.

Histories of the castle say that its blackest period was during the time that it was used as a Covenanter prison. In May 1684, 122 men and 45 women were sent here accused of recusancy (basically not acknowledging the authority of the King over the Church). Sir Walter Scott said they were driven to the castle 'like a flock of bullocks' and herded together in a cellar, soon to be known as the 'Whig's Vault'. It will come as no surprise that they were not treated terribly well. Light came in through one window but, unfortunately, so did the wind and rain. Soon the prisoners were wading through two feet of muck – much of it their own, for they had no access 'to ease of nature', as one historian has so delicately put it. If they had money they could bribe the guards for small luxuries, like food and water, otherwise they were left to starve and die of thirst.

Although some of these recusants were eventually moved to slightly better accommodation, others decided they'd had enough of this treatment and tried to escape through the window and along a narrow ledge. Local women saw them and raised the alarm but by then 25 had escaped. Eventually 15 of the weakest were recaptured. The King's men beat them and dragged them back to the castle, where some were tied hand and foot and while they lay on their backs lighted tapers were placed between their fingers to burn the flesh through to the bone.

When a pregnant wife of one of these Covenanters travelled up from the south to see her husband, the governor took her prisoner and threw her into the Whig's Vault, where she later died. Finally, those prisoners left alive were transferred to Leith, where some were sold to the owner of a West Indies plantation as slave labour. However a fever struck the boat carrying them to the colonies killing the plantation

DEVIL'S GALLOP   123

owner, his wife and all the crew, apart from the captain and one other officer. The prisoners dropped at the rate of three or four a day and their bodies were casually tossed overboard. Fifteen weeks later the ship limped into port – but not Jamaica, as planned. The winds had carried the ship to New Jersey. Here the few surviving prisoners were offered their freedom. The rigours of frontier life would be nothing compared to the hell they had been through.

I left the castle and made my way to Stonehaven. The old town is clustered around its harbour. There might have been more of it left had the Marquis of Montrose not come calling in 1645 and torched the joint. He would return the following year to sail abroad – his king a prisoner and his cause lost.

Looking onto the harbour is the sixteenth-century tollbooth. It's now a museum and is the oldest building in town. It was once a storehouse used by the Earl Marischal, George Keith, and later became a prison and courthouse. Episcopal ministers were imprisoned here by Covenanters but their congregation still managed to ensure their children were baptised by holding them up to the ministers at their barred windows. There is also a house in the town that was used for meetings around 1746 by the Reverend Alexander Greig in defiance of the legislation forbidding congregations larger than five people.

Miscreants were branded in a nearby blacksmith's shop. After one such event, when a prisoner ended up getting his ears pierced, the man cried out, 'I'd be all right now if I had some pendices [earrings].' Another man was branded on the shoulder for theft and was then forced to watch a fellow prisoner hang at Dunottar for stealing cattle.

DEVIL'S GALLOP

TWENTY-FOUR

Sharp Blades and Furry Boots

Continuing along the A92 I reached the 'Granite City' of Aberdeen (so called – astonishingly – because many of the buildings are made of granite). There has been a settlement here since prehistoric times, and later invaders included the Picts, the Romans and Texas oilmen. There is not much of the old city left, but it was huddled around the areas now known as Pittodrie and Seaton. Although St Machar's Cathedral dates back to the twelfth century, houses in the area only go back to the eighteenth century.

William Wallace, rapidly becoming known as 'Torchy', put a fleet of English ships to the flame in 1297. Edward III then repaid the compliment by destroying the town. Montrose came here three times during his struggle with Cromwell and the Covenanters. During his 'Year of Miracles' in 1644, Montrose decided to visit Aberdeen and give the men of God here a quick smite. The night before he arrived, a blood-red moon rose earlier than usual. It was a portent of the terrible acts that would forever besmirch Montrose's good name.

Montrose stopped on the outskirts of the city and sent a messenger and a drummer boy ahead to demand surrender. The burgesses were ordered to evacuate 'old persons, women and children', otherwise they could expect no quarter. The Covenanter leaders replied that 'we shall be most willing to spend the last drop of our blood therein, according to the Covenant subscribed and sworn by us.' In other words, 'Away ye go and bile yer heid, Montrose.' On the way back with the reply, a Covenanter soldier ignored the flag of truce and shot down the young drummer. Montrose witnessed the murder and swore revenge. He clashed with the defenders near to the Hardgate, above the How Burn.

During the battle, one Irish soldier fighting on the Royalist side was badly wounded in the leg. Most of us would have collapsed in agony, crying out for our mammy, but these lads were made of sterner stuff. He called out for a surgeon's saw and proceeded to hack off the injured limb without benefit of anaesthetic, a nip of whisky, or even a stick to bite on. Now literally a foot soldier, he reportedly said, 'I hope my Lord Marquis will give me a horse to be a dragooner.' He then handed the amputated leg to another man and told him to 'bury that lest some hungry Scot should eat it'.

Such bravery was completely overshadowed, though, by the aftermath of the battle. Victorious Royalists disgraced themselves by looting and raping their way through the town. According to one account, they stripped men before killing them so as not to get any blood on their clothes. If a wife or daughter cried out, they were murdered too. The corpses were left to rot in the streets while the killers went on to find new victims. For three days the slaughter continued and although the body count was not nearly as high as Covenanters later claimed, it was still a shocking episode in Montrose's career. Later, these atrocities were used to justify the far greater slaughter at Philliphaugh (see Border Raid). Later, after Montrose was executed in Edinburgh, one of his arms was returned to Aberdeen, where it was displayed on top of the tollbooth for many years.

Executions were carried out in Aberdeen in a number of places. At the top of Errol Street, overlooking Pittodrie Stadium, is Gallow Hill, which was used until 1776. (The hill is also known locally as Miser's Hillie, because football supporters too mean to buy a ticket climb up here to watch the game.) In 1752, a woman who had murdered her infant child was forced to walk to Gallow Hill through the streets with the burned body of her victim in her apron.

Other executions were carried out in the city centre, on the Castlegate near the old tollbooth. Also, criminals and witches were drowned in the Pottie, near to Shore Brae in the harbour, or else at the Quayhead. Place names like 'Gallowgate', 'Heading Hill' and 'Hangman's Brig' all testify to the city's bloody past.

In 1562, Mary Queen of Scots was forced to watch the bloody execution of Sir John Gordon, who had joined his father, the Earl of Huntly, in a short-lived rebellion against her rule. These rebels were defeated at the Battle of Corrichie but the fat old Earl avoided the

headsman's sword by managing to die from a heart attack after falling from his horse. This, however, did not deter the Queen's supporters from propping his embalmed body up in a casket and putting it on trial. Sir John was unlucky enough to have a strong heart – and a strong neck, for it took many strokes to separate it from his body at the old tollbooth on 22 September of the same year. The heading block can be seen in the Tollbooth Museum.

A gallows was erected in Castle Street for the execution of Andrew Hossack on 15 June 1810 for a double murder committed some years before. The man went to his death quietly enough but insisted he was innocent. The authorities 'borrowed' the horse and cart of hangman (and former thief) Johnny Milne to transport the body to its grave on Gallow Hill. Milne was unhappy with the arrangement – or rather the lack of one, as he had known nothing of this plan. He was also unhappy with the way his daughter had been treated by the men sent to collect his cart. While Hossack's body still dangled from the rope, Milne handed in his notice. Hossack was buried near the hill but resurrectionists later stole his body. Milne, meanwhile, reconsidered his hasty resignation and continued as hangman for a few years.

But Aberdeen folk did not execute only criminals. In 1688, two dogs were hanged by the Protestant lordships because their Catholic owner had called them Calvin and Luther.

The Castlegate was also the scene of a bizarre 'Ordeal by Blood'. This was a curious belief that blood will flow from a corpse's wounds if touched by the murderer – or as in an Ayrshire case, the presence of a relative of the murderer (see Cannibal Run). James VI wrote about this concept in his latterday bestseller *Demonologie*. He said that it was as if 'the blood were crying to Heaven for revenge of the murderer'. In the eighteenth century, the body of an army batman was laid out in the Castlegate and a regiment of troops forced to march past and touch the corpse in an effort to find the killer. Needless to say, nothing happened, apart from a lot of soldiers rushing to scrub their hands.

TWENTY-FIVE
In Like Flynn

I left Aberdeen and kept heading north on the A92 but eventually turned onto the A975. A fine rain sprayed the air as I reached the tiny bay-side village of Collieston, once a hotbed of smugglers. The sea caves north and south of this randomly laid-out little port proved very useful to those freebooting adventurers who defied the excise men to bring home brandy for the parson and baccy for the clerk. The trade reached its peak here between 1660 and 1690, although it was common until the early nineteenth century. It was then estimated that 8,000 gallons of spirits from the continent were landed tax-free every month.

One local man who smuggled his way through life was Philip Kennedy. He was ambushed by excisemen near here on 19 December 1798 and a fight ensued for possession of the goods. His gang took fright and scarpered but Kennedy fought on, eventually taking a deep cutlass slash to the head. He managed to make his way north to Slains kirkyard where he died.

Also at Collieston I found St Catherine's Dubh, a rocky inlet where the Spanish vessel *Santa Katarina* sank around 1590. It was believed the ship was bringing arms to Francis Hay, who had angered James VI by not taking Protestantism to his bosom. Hay was one of the Earls of Errol and their base was Slain Castle, which sits on the rocks some distance to the north of Collieston. The castle is now little more than a finger of stone thanks to James who had it destroyed in 1594 after his victory over the forces of Catholicism at the battle of Glenlivet. By 1664, the Errol Earls had built themselves a new fortress near Cruden Bay, further along the A975 – which by a strange coincidence just happened to be my next stop.

Thanks to a championship course, Cruden Bay is now a popular

DEVIL'S GALLOP

spot for golfers but in the Victorian age it was a favourite resort for the rich and famous, who came to stay in a high-class railway hotel, which has now gone. I made my way down to Port Errol harbour, by the great arc of golden sands that fringes the bay, and climbed up the hill to a stretch of waste ground peppered with decaying buildings dating from the Second World War. A lady out walking her dog told me that this place was once a golf course too, although there's no sign of that now. Seabirds dipped and wheeled among the cliffs of red granite, crying to each other against the wind. T.E. Lawrence, who visited this area, called their sound 'the saddest, most cold disembodied voices in the world'. There are herons here too – those great, grey creatures that look prehistoric in flight. But nature study was not what brought me here. The object of my visit was looming in the late evening gloom and fine rain across a rocky chasm – the ruins of Slains Castle. You can't reach the castle from here, by the way. To do so, you must go through the town and park in a small area past a ruined farm steading. Then it's a fairly short walk along a track to the castle. However, the building is dangerous and visitors are strongly advised not to go too close.

This sixteenth-century ruin was quite some shack in its day. Dr Johnson and his sidekick James Boswell wrote some nice things about the castle and its clifftop views. Boswell also claimed to have seen the ghost of Lord Kilmarnock (the then Lord Errol's father) who had been beheaded at London's Tower Hill in 1746 for his part in the Jacobite uprising. However in 1916, with the family fortunes in sharp decline, the castle was sold to a shipping magnate who had it partially torn down.

In 1893, Abraham 'Bram' Stoker, an Irish-born theatrical manager, was on holiday at Peterhead when he first discovered Cruden Bay. He liked what he saw and decided to decamp to the town's Kilmarnock Arms Hotel (which is still standing). This was the first of many visits to the resort and it was during one such trip that he wrote the first parts of the book that would make him a household name – *Dracula*, published in 1897. They say Slains Castle provided inspiration, but of course in those days it was still a bustling house and very far from the image of Castle Dracula. Stoker went on to set three other short stories in the area and, with his *Dracula* royalties, bought himself a house nearby – the Crookit Lum in Whinnyfold across the bay. Stoker is still remembered in the area, even though he has been dead for almost 90 years. I received some cold looks and exasperated shakes of the head in Whinnyfold when I asked which house was his, but in Cruden Bay I was told that the grandfather of a local doctor had treated the writer during one of his stays. In gratitude, Stoker presented him with a silver cigarette case, which is still in the family.

A later member of the Hay family has a place in the dark hall of infamy too, although it was for an incident that took place thousands of miles away from the harsh winds and misty rain of the Buchan coast. Josslyn Hay was the 22nd Earl of Errol. In January 1941 he was shot and killed in Kenya. He was an old African hand, having lived there since 1923 (although he called his bungalow Slains) and at the time of his death was Military Secretary. The murder brought to light some pretty raunchy goings-on among the ex-patriate Brits that were detailed in James Fox's book *White Mischief*. The murder remains unsolved, although the husband of one of the victim's many consorts did stand trial and was acquitted.

I stayed the night in Cruden Bay and in the morning, under skies dark and glowering, I continued on the A975 until its junction with the A952, when I turned left towards Aberdeen. But I was not returning to the Granite City. After two days of travelling north I was now heading westwards: through Buchan and Moray, towards the heathery field which signified the end of the Jacobite dream.

TWENTY-SIX

Battle Lines

In Ellon, I looked for signs for the A920 and Old Meldrum. It was just outside this place, on the B9170 road to Inverurie, that Robert the Bruce met the Earl of Buchan in battle. Buchan's family traditionally had no love for the Bruce clan. And the fact that Robert had stabbed his nephew (the Red Comyn) in a Dumfries church prior to seizing the crown of Scotland did not help.

Buchan camped here, on Barra Hill, which rises to the left of the road. Bruce was based at Inverurie a few miles to the south. In May 1308 they clashed around what is now the Inverurie road. Buchan's troops, although they outnumbered Bruce's, were routed and he made post-haste for England. Bruce then embarked on the programme of burning, murdering and looting known as the 'Herschip of Buchan'.

I travelled the length of the B9170 to Inverurie, to find the site of another battle – one of the few that ended in a draw (albeit a bloody one). I drove through the town until I joined the main A96, turning right towards Inverness. After I had left the last house of the town behind, I took the first right turn (marked for Harlaw) onto a small single-track road until I reached a church. I made another right turn here and could see the monument tower.

The cause of this brutal confrontation between Highland host and Lowland army had its roots in a bit of marital skulduggery and disputes over land. Now pay attention, for this gets a bit complicated. James III was in captivity in England and Moray was Regent. When the Earl of Ross died, Moray convinced the dead man's daughter Euphemia to cede the lands to her uncle, the Earl of Buchan. Euphemia then promptly took herself to a nunnery. There was, however, a rival claimant to the lands of Ross, and that was Donald MacDonald, Lord of the Isles, who had married the late Earl's sister.

Not surprisingly, Moray rejected MacDonald's claim. (The fact that Buchan was Moray's son may well have been a factor in his decision.)

In a separate development, Alexander Stewart, son of the notorious Wolf of Badenoch (more on him later), had his eyes on the rich lands of Mar, west of Aberdeen. First he killed the Earl, then courted his widow – not by buying her flowers and complimenting her hair, but by the powers of persuasion he had inherited from his vicious father – in other words, threats and sieges. So when MacDonald set out to take Ross by force, raiding Inverness then turning eastwards to head for Aberdeen, it was the new Earl of Mar who stepped in to stop him. He had the Aberdeen authorities raise a small army, which he led west to meet the approaching MacDonalds. The two armies met at Harlaw on 24 July 1411.

The subsequent battle was a nasty, brutish affair with each side simply lunging at the other across the heath. The Highlanders' famous charge – in which the kilted warrior runs at the enemy, claymore held high, screaming his clan war-cry at the top of his lungs – proved ineffective against the tightly-packed knot of Lowland spearmen. The MacDonald men soon found themselves impaled on pike points and left bleeding on the ground. However, when the Highlanders did break through they spilled so much blood on the ground that the battle became known as 'Red Harlaw'. Through the day and into the night the two sides hacked, stabbed and gouged at one another until finally the MacDonalds and their allies left the battlefield while Mar's rag-tag army of Lowland knights and Aberdeen citizens limped back east. Neither side could legitimately claim victory and the only losers in what was little more than a family dispute were the 1,500 corpses whose blood had stained the land red. The huge monument recalls Aberdeen Provost Robert Davidson, Alexander Irvine of Drum and Hector McLean of Duart who all perished during this great bloody confrontation.

Heading back along the narrow road to the A96, I once again turned in the direction of Inverness. Just before Huntly, I passed the small village of Slioch, where, prior to his defeat at the Hill of Barra, the Comyn Earl of Buchan first encountered Bruce's troops. This took place on Christmas Day 1307 but the hostilities amounted to little more than some name-calling and the odd arrow or two. Bruce took ill here, and was carried to Huntly Castle, which lies on the outskirts of

DEVIL'S GALLOP

the village of the same name just a bit further along the A96. In Bruce's day, the castle was a wooden structure known as Strathbogie. This changed after Bannockburn because the then Laird had made the mistake of siding with the English. The lands were handed over to the Gordons of Huntly.

In January 1496, James IV witnessed a spectacular wedding here, when his cousin Lady Catherine Gordon, known as the White Rose of Scotland, married the strangely named Perkin Warbeck, who claimed to be one of the princes in the tower supposedly murdered by the evil Richard III. He was actually the offspring of a Flemish customs officer, but Lady Gordon believed his story. When Henry VII captured them both he forced Warbeck to confess all and she turned her back on him. The imposter was eventually hanged at Tyburn, his head chopped off and spiked on old London Bridge.

It was a Huntly who conspired against Mary Queen of Scots but died of a heart attack before he could be executed. Just before that, Mary had planned to spend the night here during a tour of her northern kingdom but changed her mind at the last minute, not trusting Huntly as far as she could throw him – and as he tended to the rotund side that was not nearly far enough. Her decision proved fortuitous for it was later revealed that the arrogant cock o' the north had planned to abduct her. The Queen travelled to Inverness instead and found herself harassed along the way by Huntly's men.

It was another Huntly who joined forces with the Earl of Erroll when he went 'in like Flynn' against the Reformation. James VI blew holes in the castle after that, using gunpowder supplied by the city of Aberdeen. Later, though, they must have made up since James used Huntly to bring down the troublesome Earl of Moray, who had apparently joined forces with the hated Francis, Earl of Bothwell. It was rumoured that the handsome Moray was the Queen's 'bonnie lover' and this irked Huntly, who also fancied himself as something of a matinee idol. Huntly caught up with Moray at Donibristle Castle, on the north coast of the Forth and hacked at his face. 'Ye hae spoiled a better face than your ain, my Lord,' said Moray just before Huntly's men butchered him. The King was angered over the killing, for he had wanted Moray alive, and he punished the errant Huntly with a full week's imprisonment in Edinburgh Castle.

It was yet another Huntly who supported Charles against the Covenanters. Montrose – at that time on the side of the sharp-faced men of God – arrested him at Inverurie and he went to his death at Edinburgh, famously telling his executioners, 'You may take my head from my shoulders, but not my heart from my sovereign.'

On a quieter note, the castle still boasts an elaborate frontispece over the door to the main building, which has somehow managed to survive the various tribulations visited upon the structure. Meanwhile, on a plaster wall near the prison in the basement, there are some fine examples of sixteenth-century graffiti.

Leaving Huntly and heading towards Inverness on the A96, I noted that the countryside here is fat and green with fine hardwood trees and ubiquitous conifers. But there was a hint here and there of the wildness that was to come. I was in Moray now and a sign told me that it was Malt Whisky Country. Keith, I was told, is the 'Friendly Town' although Gypsy James MacPherson did not find it so – for it was here that he was captured after a lifetime of banditry. He was notorious in the area, as much for his robberies as his escapes from prison.

In 1700, MacPherson was attending the famed Summer Eve's Fair, which took place in the large square in the centre of the old town. He was recognised by William Duff, Laird of Braco, and arrested. But followers of Duff's rival, the Laird of Grant, wanted the honour of capturing the famed robber themselves and there followed a most unseemly stand-off. Eventually, MacPherson and his men were taken to jail in Banff (to the north-east) and subsequently sentenced to hang. According to legend, the local authorities heard that MacPherson was to receive a last minute reprieve and put the town clock forward one hour so he could dangle before the official word reached them. He actually died on the morning of Friday 16 November 1700, even though he was sentenced to go to the gallows between two and three in the afternoon. But this may have been simply because the local magistrates were worried he would be sprung by his gang at the last minute.

His final wish was to play his fiddle one last time, and the sweet tones of the self-composed 'MacPherson's Rant' filled the air. He then asked the crowd if anyone would take his fiddle and play it at his wake.

DEVIL'S GALLOP

When no one came forward MacPherson smashed the instrument against his knee, placed his head in the noose and stepped off the ladder without assistance from the hangman. The neck of the fiddle is now in the possession of the Clan MacPherson while Robert Burns immortalised the bandit in the poem 'MacPherson's Farewell'.

TWENTY-SEVEN

Hubble, Bubble, Toil
and Iambic Pentameter

I pressed on, through the town of Fochabers, and into Elgin, where fact and Shakespearean fiction collide. Shakespeare's *Macbeth* makes Gibson's *Braveheart* look like a documentary. According to the Bearded Bard of Avon, Macbeth was a guilt-racked, murderous monarch driven by a near demonic queen into reaching further than he could grasp before finally coming to grief at the hands of the true king, Malcolm Canmore.

Actually, Macbeth was a 'Celtic Mormaer', or 'High Steward', of Moray, who rebelled against Duncan, who was not the old, much-loved man of the Scottish play but a young king who had ruled unpopularly for six years. His grandfather had changed the right of succession to put him on the throne and that irked other claimants, including Macbeth. Here, at Elgin, Macbeth's forces were victorious in battle and Duncan retired to his castle on Ladyhill overlooking the town to die from his wounds. The scant remains of a later stone castle can be seen on the hill around the base of the 80 foot high Doric column that supports a statue to the fifth Duke of Gordon.

Macbeth held the kingdom for 16 years before finally being killed by Malcolm at Lumphanan in Aberdeenshire. However, Shakespeare's version of the legend has taken hold in the area, for a hill to the west of Elgin, known as the 'Knock O' Alves' is said to be where the future king met the three witches.

The Wolf of Badenoch came to Elgin to protest forcibly about his excommunication by the Bishop of Moray. Alexander Stewart was the bastard son of Robert II (although the King did marry his mother, Elizabeth Muir, a few years after the boy was born). In 1371, the

young man received the title Lord of Badenoch, once in Comyn ownership, but swiftly became known as the 'Wolf' because, according to one account, 'He was cruel and merciless . . . sparing none.'

He operated a protection racket in which he promised to spare the lands of neighbouring nobles as long as they paid him a levy. The Bishop of Moray refused to pay this, then went on to criticise Badenoch's decision to leave his wife for another woman. Refusing the duty was one thing, but criticising his sex life was another, so in 1390 the Wolf and his pack rode out of their stronghold at Lochindorb Castle and howled north. They burned Forres, then attacked Elgin Cathedral – said then to be the most beautiful in Scotland. The Bishop was so outraged that he excommunicated the Wolf.

Twelve years later, another raider plundered the rich cathedral: Alexander MacDonald, son of the Lord of the Isles. A few months afterwards, he and his wild Highlanders returned for more booty but this time they were met at the gates by the Bishop who preached with such passion that they fell to their knees and begged to be forgiven. There is a cross in nearby College Street that was erected by MacDonald by way of apology.

In a deep pool of water to the east of the cathedral, the local worthies used to drown witches. The pool was known as the 'Order', or 'Ordeal', pot. The Elgin witches could think themselves lucky, for further along the A96, at Forres, the good people had something worse in store for their kind. The Witches Stone sits by the roadway just in front of the police station. It's not very big and easily missed, so the best way to see it is to park a few yards further on and walk back. Macbeth may have occupied the castle here but the ruins on Castle Hill are unlikely to be that old. James VI visited this place in 1600 and on his way back south took ill at Scone, suffering a malady caused, it was believed, by witchcraft. Sure enough, enquiries revealed a coven operating in Forres, caught in the act of melting a wax image of the King. Or so the authorities claimed. The witches were dragged to the top of Cluny Hill (where there is now a memorial to Lord Nelson) and bent double into barrels of tar which were then rolled downhill. The barrels were burnt where they stopped and the stone marks the spot where at least one of them came to rest. It was cracked centuries later while being removed during construction work.

DEVIL'S GALLOP

Forres is also the home of Sueno's Stone, which stands on a side road further back towards the A96 (there are signposts). This 23-foot high, intricately-carved sandstone slab is of mysterious origin, and its images of warriors and headless corpses may depict a battle fought by the Danish warrior Sueno (or Sweyn) against the local Picts. Or it may not. Whatever it shows, the stone – even encased in its transparent tomb as it is now – is hugely impressive, yet not very well known in Scotland. One expert has dubbed it 'one of the most remarkable Dark Age sculptured stones in Britain, if not in Europe'.

Leaving Forres, I made my way back to the A96, following signs for Nairn, although I planned to turn off before reaching the town. In Auldearn I followed signs for the Boath Doocot, a National Trust property marking the spot where Montrose raised his standard during a battle fought in the fields near to the town. The signs petered out soon after I entered a tidy residential area and it was only by luck that I spotted another, partially obscured by bushes, pointing to the doocot site at the far end of a public garden.

The doocot, standing on a mound behind some trees, dates back to the seventeenth century and signifies the landed gentry's love of pigeons (or at least their flesh, for pigeon pie was a fancy dainty). This particular doocot was built on Castle Hill, the site of an old royal castle, some years after Montrose came with his Royalist forces in May 1645. The Covenanting forces, under General Hurry, had swiftly marched eastwards from Inverness to surprise him. Montrose, who throughout his campaign showed a deplorable grasp of the enemy's movements, had no idea Hurry was so close and was almost caught with his pantaloons down. For a while it looked as if things were going badly for the Royalists – with the Irish MacDonalds, under Alastair McColla supported by Gordons, taking the brunt of the attack. But McColla did not like taking the defensive position so he led his men on the offensive and onto the points of the Covenanter pikemen. McColla fought like the wild man he was and when enemy pikes embedded themselves in his targe (Highland shield) he simply sliced through them with his great sword and fought on.

One MacDonald was shot in the mouth with an arrow. Although the point pierced his tongue and plunged through his cheek he still battled – first with a pistol, before attempting to draw his sword, which was somehow stuck in its scabbard. While he struggled with the handle, he took the points of five pikes in the chest but still he remained on his feet.

In a hollow unseen by the Covenanting forces, Montrose waited with the Gordon cavalry. When told that things were going badly for McColla's troops, Montrose turned and said, 'Come, my Lord Gordon, what are we waiting for? Our friend MacDonald on the right has routed the enemy and is slaughtering the fugitives. Shall we look on idly and let him carry off the honours of the day?' They charged and Montrose added another victory to his Year of Miracles.

I left this battlefield to head for one that is infinitely more famous. It was the last full battle to be fought on British soil and its aftermath brought a severe backlash from an angry government onto the Highlands. The dream of a return of the Stuarts to the throne had begun in earnest when Bonnie Prince Charlie landed on the West Coast. It took shape when his standard was raised at Glenfinnan. It gathered momentum at Prestonpans. It suffered a reversal during the retreat from Derby when the promised English support was not forthcoming. And it died on the heather of Drummossie Moor – better known to history as Culloden.

TWENTY-EIGHT

Where the Wind Sighs

The thing I remember most about Culloden is the silence. A road runs past what is left of the battlefield but somehow the sound of the cars, lorries and buses did not penetrate. All I heard was the sigh of the wind through the heather and the occasional startled cry of a grouse in the bracken.

This was where the Stuart dream perished on a cold, sleet-filled day in April 1746. Prince Charles Edward Stuart, ignoring the advice of wiser counsel, chose to meet Cumberland's seasoned troops on bleak Drummossie Moor; soft, marshy land unsuitable for the Highland charge but ideally suited to the disciplined tactics of the British regulars. His men were tired and under-fed, worn out from an attempted night raid against the enemy, from which they had returned without even catching sight of their quarry. They were also outnumbered, numbering only 5,000, while Cumberland had 9,000 troops, many of them battle-seasoned veterans. But the clans would fight, for that was what they did best. They had proven their mettle – first at Prestonpans and later at Falkirk. They had forced their way into England as far as Derby and sent panic pulsing through London. However the failure of English Jacobites to rally to their cause, disagreements between generals, the presence of a weak and petulant prince at their head and intrigue by English spies had forced them to retreat north.

The fighting began at 1 p.m. on 16 April with an exchange of cannon fire. One rebel cannonball narrowly missed the Duke of Cumberland – no mean feat, for he was not a small man. But the rebel artillery was no match for the well-trained British guns and soon the Jacobite cannons fell silent, their gunners dead or fled. The British cannons were then turned onto the Highland lines. Volley after volley

DEVIL'S GALLOP

was fired into the clansmen as they waited with growing impatience for the order to charge. Men fell in droves; blown apart by the lethal cannon fire or flesh torn to shreds by grapeshot. And still the order did not come. Behind them, Charles dithered and ignored the pleas from his generals to allow the men to charge, or at least to give them some chance, rather than just let them stand around waiting to be killed. But still he hesitated and the order did not come. Finally, the men of Clan MacIntosh and Clan Chattan could take the carnage no longer and roared across the 400 yards of heather towards the enemy, the wind and sleet stinging at their faces, with Atholl Highlanders and Camerons racing up to the rear. Now it was the turn of the redcoat soldiers to wreak bloody havoc. Blistering volleys of musket fire ripped into the charging Highlanders; the bullets singing out of the cannon smoke and felling the rebels as they blundered forward. Those who did make it to the disciplined lines found that the English had worked out a new way of bayonet fighting: thrusting not at the man in front, but the man to the right, thereby avoiding the hard targe and striking deep under the raised sword arm.

A Highlander, John McGillivray, forced his way through the first line, killing 12 men before he was brought down. Another Highlander, wounded and lying against earth dykes threw himself at a troop of English soldiers, killing 13 before he himself was cut down. Cumberland witnessed this brave act and wished the man's life had been spared, although he had given the order that no quarter was to be given.

The MacDonalds were smarting after the Prince failed to place them on their traditional position on the right flank. One of their chiefs, MacDonald of Keppoch, was hit as he charged, crying, 'My God, have the clansmen of my name deserted me?' His men, stung by the rebuke, followed him into the carnage.

Alisdair MacGillivray of Clan Chattan had crawled to a small spring for water and was shot dead as he drank. His head fell into the pool, while around him fellow rebels were cut down. Later, the stream was found to be choked with dead Scotsmen and it became known as the 'Well of the Dead' – and woe betide anyone who drank from its waters.

There were Scots fighting on the Hanoverian side, for this was civil war and families could be ripped apart by divided loyalties. In this way, it was hoped families would continue to prosper no matter which side won. Roderick, the youngest son of the chief of Clan Chisholm for instance, was a Jacobite, but his two brothers fought on the government side. A cannonball struck down the young man and his brother found his body. They say that the black chanter of the clan could not play if a member of the chief's family was to die. No one can say for certain if the clan piper, Ian Beg, could draw a note at Culloden.

Campbells, loyal to the Crown, had found themselves a vantage point behind the walls of the Culwhiniac Enclosure and from there they let loose a volley of gunfire against their countrymen, blasting the heart out of the Atholl clan. And as the Highlanders retreated, the Argyll men leaped over the walls and hacked at them with their own claymores. Meanwhile, at a barn near old Leannach Cottage, wounded Jacobite officers were burned alive by soldiers when they tried to take shelter.

Charles was led away by his advisors, the furious words of Lord Elcho ringing in his ears. This young Scottish lord had commanded the Prince's guard and as he saw his Prince being taken away, he cried, 'Run, you cowardly Italian!'

By the time the battle was over, in just over an hour, nearly 1,200 clansmen lay dead on the moor – along with around 200 British troops. The Highlanders were buried in trenches on the field, the sites indicated by a series of markers with the clan names etched on them. According to legend, no heather will grow over the graves, while rowan trees protect them from evil. A field where the redcoat dead were buried is marked simply: 'the Field of the English'.

The battle was over but the slaughter continued. Redcoated troops roamed the moor, bayoneting wounded Highlanders. Patrols caught up with those fleeing the field and shot them where they stood. Innocent civilians were murdered as the blood-lust rose. Such is the everlasting shame about these actions that no regiment today lists Culloden among its battle honours.

The atrocities continued for months as a determined government stamped out any further thoughts of rebellion, and hunted for the fugitive prince. Tartan was banned, the pipes outlawed, the people

DEVIL'S GALLOP

beaten into submission. Within 100 years, the Highland way of life would be nothing but a memory. The Highland Clearances finished off what the heavy hand of Butcher Cumberland had begun.

Part of the battlefield is preserved now, although its fringes are constantly under threat from development. I heard an American woman asking a guide whether there were any hard feelings against Prince Charlie for the disaster. She was told that the only hard feelings are reserved for the English. For my money, the memory of Charles Edward Stuart should not be honoured in Scotland, for it was his greed and petulance that brought the clans to the debacle at Drummossie Moor, his disregard for their health and well-being that killed them. I think that if he had listened to experienced men like Lord George Murray then perhaps the result would have been different. Although he has gone into history as a romantic hero, largely due to his adventures after Culloden while dodging the English patrols combing the Highlands for him, Scots should rue the day he ever came to these shores.

Feeling oddly subdued, I left the killing-field of Culloden to spend the night in Inverness, where prisoners bore the brunt of Cumberland's wrath following the battle.

TWENTY-NINE
Highland Capital

There is not much of old Inverness left, apart from the Old High Kirk in Church Street. It was here that Jacobite prisoners were made to sit on a small headstone while redcoats knelt by another stone nearby, rested the barrels of their muskets in a hollow carved on the top and shot them.

The town suffered greatly after the battle, as soldiers, their blood up, continued to hack and kill in the streets. The late John Prebble, in his masterful book *Culloden*, tells of the first trooper to enter the town cutting the throats of two men in a house near the old tollbooth, which stood at the foot of the Castle Wynd. Prisoners were herded into the churchyards and gaols, into cellars and lofts, and into the stinking holds of ships anchored on the Moray Firth. They died in their hundreds from untended wounds and from sickness brought on by the filthy conditions.

There was another cell in the old bridge across the River Ness. On good days it was half-filled with water; on bad days the rats came to nip and nibble. One person jailed by vengeful English officers was Anne McKay who was accused of helping two Jacobites escape. She lay in the foetid pit, and refused the strong drink sent to her in an effort to get her so drunk she would confess her crime and implicate others. Finally, someone took pity on her and allowed her to leave.

Eventually, those prisoners who survived were shipped off – for execution, for transportation to the colonies or to a living hell on prison hulks on the Thames.

English deserters were marched to an execution point just outside town, stripped and hanged from a gibbet, their bodies mutilated afterwards. One Scot, who began fighting for King George but who changed sides, was executed while wearing an officer's uniform he had

stolen – on the direct orders of Cumberland, who thought it a jolly wheeze.

And then there is the story of Murdoch McRaw, arrested as a Jacobite simply because others of his name had fought for Charlie. After a ludicrous trial, he was taken to an apple tree at the town cross, all the time believing it was a joke. As they placed the noose around his neck, he said, 'You have gone far enough if this be jest.' But this was no laughing matter, at least not for him. He was tipped off the ladder and left to hang for two days, while soldiers whipped his dead body for fun. Finally, he was cut down and buried by beggars press-ganged into disposing of the dead. But they say the tree died that day, and produced no more fruit.

The town cross where this happened can still be seen in front of the Town Hall on Bridge Street, near Castle Wynd. At its foot is a bluish stone known as 'Clach na Cuddin' which they say is the old coronation stone of the MacDonalds, Lords of the Isles. If anything was the centre of town life this was it. Here the women paused to gossip with their washing on their way from the river while the men folk thrashed out trade deals.

At the top of the Wynd is the red sandstone bulk of the Gothic castle, built in 1834 and now used as a sheriff court. There has been a castle on or near this site since the twelfth century and according to legend it is (one of the many sites) where Macbeth allegedly slew Duncan. Macbeth probably did rule the province of Moray from here but his fortress, made of wood, was a few hundred yards to the north east of this place.

In 1428, the northern lords felt the weight of Stewart anger when James I called 40 of them to a parliament convened at Inverness. He wanted to subdue them and had them immediately thrown into the castle dungeons. In an admirable feat of self-control for a king (and a Stewart), he hanged only three of them – just to make a point. However, it failed to impress Alexander MacDonald, Lord of the Isles, who came back later and burned the town. James then captured Alexander and forced him to appear before him in Edinburgh clad only in his underclothes, to pledge allegiance. MacDonald was then sent to Tantallon Castle as a prisoner.

Later, in 1562, Mary Queen of Scots visited Inverness Castle when

Lord Gordon of Huntly was up to his rebellious tricks. One of Huntly's sons refused to let her in and so the Queen was forced to find lodgings in a house at the bottom of the hill on Bridge Street. It all ended happily for the Queen, for when Huntly heard the Inverness people were in support of her he sent word to his son to let her in. It didn't end quite so happily for Huntly Junior whose head was duly removed from his body.

In 1724, General Wade, that famed road builder, extended the fort. But in 1746, Jacobites used those roads and blew it up. All that remains of the old structure is a well and part of one wall. There is, however, now a museum here called The Garrison Encounter, which promises to take visitors back to those dark and bloody days of 1745–46 when they can accept the king's shilling and find out what life was like for a common soldier under Cumberland. Accepting a flogging is optional, presumably.

In front of the castle is a statue of Flora MacDonald, one of the many heroines of the Jacobite era. It was Flora who smuggled Charles Edward Stuart from Benbecula over the sea to Skye while the English searched desperately for him. At first she was unwilling to become one of Charlie's angels, but once committed, she really took charge. She talked the Prince into disguising himself as maid servant Betty Burke and spirited him away to relative safety. Later, she was imprisoned in the Tower of London but the Prince of Wales took a liking to her and set her free. She married, moved to the Americas and had a squad of youngsters before returning to her home in Skye where she died. The statue at Inverness shows her with her hand at her eyes, shielding them from the sun, while a faithful dog looks up at her.

From this statue, I looked across the river towards the twin spires of St Andrew's Cathedral and the tree-covered hump of Tomnahurich behind it. This is Inverness's famed 'hill of the fairies', although now it's also a hill of death for it is the site of one of Scotland's most beautiful cemeteries. But the fairies are still there, they say, unafraid of Man's burial rites and traditions. On dark nights the unwary walker can hear the scampering of tiny feet and the shrill cry of fairy pipes. They say two local men who were entranced by the sound and joined the party awoke to find themselves in an Inverness one hundred years in the future.

A riot broke out near the castle here during the local Marymas fair in August 1665 – and it was all over the price of cheese. It began when one Finlay Dhu asked the price of a block of cheese at a stall. When the woman behind the counter told him the cost, he either dropped it from shock or threw it away in disgust. Whatever happened the cheese rolled down the hill. The woman gave him the benefit of her extended knowledge of epithets, to which Finlay took exception. An argument developed, sides were taken, swords drawn and blood spilled. This in turn alerted the Town Guard, which prompted yet more blades to be unsheathed. Although there were no fatalities, a number of people were injured in the street fight.

THIRTY
Barracks Life

I left Inverness on a bright, clear day and began my trek southwards on the infamous A9, which cuts through the heart of Scotland as far as Stirling before side-stepping to Edinburgh. They say this is one of the most lethal roads in Scotland but there are no dangerous roads, just dangerous drivers. And you see them here, roaring past you at great speed, leap-frogging traffic with alarming frequency. The road veers between single and dual carriageway and you can be toodling along merrily on what you think is the outside lane only to find yourself suddenly playing chicken with an oncoming juggernaut.

The landscape here is considerably different from that of the east coast. It's rugged and mountainous with vast stretches of bleak moorland stretching to faraway hills. I travelled a fair distance before I reached my next port of call.

I passed the skiing centre of Aviemore and reached the town of Kingussie, which boasts a fine Highland Folk Museum where visitors can feel what it was like to sit in an old black house and have fumes from the peat fire sting the eyes. In the neighbouring town of Newtonmore is the Clan MacPherson Museum, where you can see the famed 'Black Chanter'.

But I was here to see Ruthven Barracks, which stand on a hill to the left of the A9 but are reached by driving through Kingussie on the right. The Wolf of Badenoch once occupied a fortress on this natural mound. According to legend, a tall, black-clad man visited him and they played a game of chess that lasted for many hours. Finally, the dark man won the game and rose from the table. As if on cue, a tremendous thunderstorm erupted outside that lasted all night. The next morning, the Wolf's men were found outside the castle walls, their bodies black and burned, as if struck by lightning. The Wolf himself lay dead in his great hall, the iron nails of his boots mysteriously torn out, although his body was unmarked. The dark man, of course, was the Devil and the game of chess was a Bergmanesque battle for the Wolf's soul. Although he had been allowed back into the Church, the Devil took him for his past deeds. Further storms raged when it came to bury him and his men and these did not abate until Badenoch's body was taken to the rear of the funeral procession.

The Devil was one of the few who did manage to penetrate the defences of this fortress. In 1592, the Clan Chattan laid siege to the place while the Gordons of Huntly held it. Angus MacIntosh led the raiders but could win by 'neither force or fraude', so he paused to reflect on his strategy. One night, a Huntly soldier crept out and indulged in a bit of sniping, aiming at a man in a yellow war-coat and killing him. This turned out to be Angus himself and his men took him away, concealing the death for many years by pretending he had gone overseas. (And the moral of that story is that next time you are besieging a castle, don't walk about at night wearing yellow.)

Two years later, the castle was again under siege, this time by the Earl of Arran, who eventually gave up and headed off east for the scrap at Glenlivet.

The site was used as a barracks for the first time in 1689, when government troops were garrisoned here, only to surrender to the forces of Bonnie Dundee, who left the building a smoking ruin. The present barracks were built to discourage further Jacobite uprisings after the 1715 unpleasantness and were extended by General Wade during his road building programme of 1724. In 1745 the Jacobites did in fact rise again and attacked the barracks. They were at the time defended by a stubborn Irishman, Sergeant Terence Molloy, and 14 men. Two hundred hairy Highlanders assaulted the walls but were repulsed by the tiny garrison. The attackers offered to let the men go free but Molloy told them – in the words of his own report to General Sir John Cope – 'I was too old a soldier to surrender a garrison of such strength without bloody noses.' Neither side had any heavy artillery – if they had the result would have been quite different – and the only real damage was to the main gate when the Jacobites tried to set it aflame. The Highlanders lost about four men. Molloy lost only one, who had made the mistake of sticking his head just a touch too far over the parapet.

In February 1746, Molloy, now promoted to Lieutenant for his valour, had to defend the barracks once more when 300 Jacobites came back for another crack at the walls. This time they brought cannons and Molloy was forced to make an honourable surrender. The rebels set fire to the barracks, destroying the roof. They would be back – although their last visit would be infinitely more touching.

After the bloody defeat at Culloden, the Highland army scattered and many of those who were not captured or murdered afterwards made their way to the old barracks. Two to three thousand men instinctively rallied here, among them Lord George Murray, the Scottish commander snubbed by the Prince before the battle. Although beaten, they were eager to regroup and have another go at the government forces. Murray had received word that clans who had remained neutral were now ready to come out for the Prince. Upward of 9,000 men could have been mustered to carry on the struggle, but Charlie was having none of it. Whether the bloodbath of Culloden had knocked the stuffing out of him, whether he realised he was not the man to lead the brave Highlanders, or whether he at last understood that his cause was lost is unclear, but he sent word to the men waiting at Ruthven: 'Let everyone seek his own safety in the best way he can.' Deserted by the Prince so many of their countrymen had died for, the Highlanders dispersed. In the words of Chevalier de Johnson, a Scottish gentleman from the Lowlands, 'The Highlanders gave vent to their grief in wild howlings and lamentations; the tears flowed down their cheeks when they thought that their country was now at the discretion of the Duke of Cumberland.'

I left Ruthven, the melancholy I had experienced at Culloden returning. The '45 Rebellion may have lasted a little more than a year over 250 years ago but the terrible cost can still be felt in the air at the battlesite and again here at Ruthven. It may be my over-active imagination, but I think there are ghostly sounds in the air at both places: at Culloden, the screams of the dying, and at Ruthven the howls of the desperate men as they realised their cause was lost, once and for all. The barracks may not be as well known a Jacobite site as the battlefield near Inverness, but the history is just as potent.

In a sombre mood, I drove back through Kingussie, onto the A9 and with a final glance at the barracks, faced southwards again.

DEVIL'S GALLOP

THIRTY-ONE

More Battle Lines

It had been my intention to find and photograph the Wade Stone, which commemorates the great road-builder and lies beside the A9. But there was a dearth of signposts and I zoomed past it before I realised it was there. The A9 at this point is a dual carriageway and there was no hope of turning back. Anyone who wants to see it can find it on the south-bound side just after the Drumochter Pass.

After a number of miles the landscape changed from the harsh browns of the heathery hills to the soft greens of the lands of Atholl. The lands around Blair Atholl Castle and Pitlochry are some of the most beautiful in Scotland, mixing the rural and the rugged into one picturesque whole. The grandiose white elegance of Blair Castle can be glimpsed to the left but it was not my destination on this trip. My next stop was a few miles further on – a deep gash cut by the River Garry known as the Pass of Killiecrankie.

The Stuart faithful of 1689, rebelling against the forces of King William, had one thing the Scots at Culloden did not have – a competent commander. James Graham of Claverhouse – Bonnie Dundee to his followers but Bloody Dundee to the Covenanters he had ruthlessly suppressed in south-west Scotland – was one of three men who could weld the Highland clans together. Montrose before him had done it and, to an extent, Charles Edward Stuart would do it too. In 1689, the Highland chiefs might have seen the struggle as a chance to level old scores or simply to enrich their coffers, but they rallied to Dundee's standard. After some successes – and a few failures – they took Blair Castle and prepared to face the oncoming enemy, here at Killicrankie.

The visitors' centre (in the care of the National Trust) is well sign-posted and offers the chance to learn about the battle and the local

DEVIL'S GALLOP 151

wildlife. After that there is a brisk walk downhill to the pass – and an even brisker walk back up. One of the first things you see is the famed 'Soldier's Leap', where Donald McBean, a redcoat trooper, is said to have escaped from Highlanders by leaping from a large, flat rock over foaming rapids to the safety of the opposite bank. The jump measures about 18 feet, so McBean was either in real fear of his life or was bionic.

The clansmen won the day at Killiecrankie. The battle itself took place on the slopes above the road but as William's troops retreated, the killing moved down to the riverbank. There is a pleasant walk here, although it's somewhat spooky as darkness falls. On the path is the Balfour Stone, where Brigadier Barthold Balfour of the redcoat Dutch Brigade was shot by an Atholl man. According to legend, the officer was buried where he fell and this stone was laid over his body. But the Highland army had its losses too, including Dundee himself, who was buried in a small chapel on the Blair Estate. I'm told there is a monument to the battle, and a battlefield viewpoint, about three kilometres from the visitors' centre in the direction of Blair Atholl. But don't hold your breath if you're looking for signposts.

Killicrankie is somewhere else I would like to have spent more time at, enjoying the air and a leisurely stroll along the riverside, but my next port of call, beyond Pitlochry, was beckoning – and it too had connections to Dundee's Jacobites.

Dunkeld is perhaps better known for its Shakespearean connections, for nearby is the village of Birnam and the wood that figured so prominently in the prophecy of Macbeth's death ('Macbeth shall never vanquish'd be until great Birnam Wood to high Dunsinane hill shall come against him.') Dunsinane, by the way, is an Iron Age hill fort lying to the south-east between Perth and Dundee. At Birnam, an oak is said to be the only survivor of the old forest of Shakespeare's time (if not Macbeth's). Dunkeld itself boasts a cathedral, where Alexander Stewart, Wolf of Badenoch is entombed. His effigy was defaced during the Reformation, as many were, but the still-visible pose of the knight on the top, his hands clasped on his breast, signifies that he died absolved of his many sins. The Devil may have taken his soul at Ruthven, but his body at least was accepted onto hallowed ground, despite his dark deeds.

DEVIL'S GALLOP

Dunkeld is another town that is under the watchful eye of the National Trust and is now a whitewashed tourist haven. Its name has been taken to mean 'the fort of the Celts', or 'the fort of the Culdees' (after an ancient Christian order). It and Scone were twin capitals of Scotland for a time during the reign of Kenneth MacAlpin in 844.

On 21 August 1689, bloodshed came to these narrow streets when 5,000 Jacobites, fresh from Killicrankie, fell on 1,200 Cameronians loyal to King William. The battle raged through the streets as William's forces fired on the clansmen from holes cut in the walls of the houses, then gradually fell back to the cathedral, setting fire to the town as they retreated. Here they repelled attack after attack, using dead Jacobites to strengthen their barricades. William Clelland, the Cameronian commander and a veteran Covenanter, was shot twice but bravely crawled out of sight so that his men could not see him die. He was later buried in the nave of the church and a memorial tablet was raised to him above the tomb of the Wolf of Badenoch.

When the Highlanders finally realised that further attack was hopeless, they withdrew, leaving what was left of the town and the cathedral to William's troops. Over 300 of their number were left dead in the streets and only 45 of the defenders had fallen. One year later, the Jacobite cause foundered when their army was defeated at the Boyne. It ended when government troops routed a small force of Jacobites at Cromdale on Speyside.

I pressed on, accomplishing what the Jacobites did not – reaching Perth. Granted, I wasn't fighting my way through determined redcoats but I was proud of myself all the same.

DEVIL'S GALLOP

THIRTY-TWO

Priory Knowledge

Perth, or 'St John's Town of Perth' as it was once known, is but a short drive down the A9 from Dunkeld. As with the other cities, the best idea is to park somewhere, buy a street map and walk around to find the sites. Which is exactly what I did.

Robert the Bruce came here in 1313, to retake it from the English. After six weeks of besieging the town walls he realised some stealth was needed. After a close inspection of the moats and the defences, he led his men away. But within a week they were back, for Bruce had worked out that men could wade across the moat at one point. The water would come up to their necks, certainly, but it was possible. And to prove it, off came his armour, his chain mail and his clothes and into the icy water he popped. Despite the fact that the notion was a bit harsh on those who were vertically challenged, his men pulled on their water wings and followed. They then scaled the walls and took the town. Whether he then slaughtered the soldiers and Scots who had welcomed the English or let them live depends on which account you believe – Scottish or English.

Wallace also came here, to attack the castle that stood at the end of what is now Skinnergate. Wallace, of course, was a bit more direct than Bruce, staging a full frontal assault and, according to Blind Harry, personally killing the captain of the guard.

My first target was the North Inch, a stretch of parkland that lies on the banks of the Tay just at the old bridge. Here, in 1396, while Robert III watched from Blackfriars Priory, members of Clan Chattan and Clan Kay faced-off against each other in a pre-arranged trial by strength in order to settle an old feud. When the two gladiatorial forces turned up, Clan Chattan was one man short and an appeal was made to the spectators for someone to take his place. A local, described as a hunch-backed, bandy-legged blacksmith, agreed to take part on the proviso that he receive 40 shillings cash and a pension for life should he survive. This was agreed and the smithy stepped into the ring. Battle commenced and all but one of the Kay side was killed. This man avoided death by leaping into the Tay and swimming to safety. Only a handful of Chattans lay dead, while the last-minute substitute, crooked back and bent legs notwithstanding, gave a sturdy account of himself.

Blackfriars Priory stood across present-day Charlotte Street and is remembered in such local street names as Blackfriars Street and Blackfriars Wynd. James I called his parliament here many times and it was hoped that the town would some day be declared the capital of Scotland. Unfortunately, an assassin's dagger put an end to that particular idea.

Although something of a poet, James was no stranger to barbarity. He had personally ordered the hanging of many a noble who stepped out of line, and on one spectacular occasion he made 300 Highland raiders dance the hangman's jig. He vowed to break the power of the barons and naturally this meant he was not on their Top Ten Favourite Monarchs list.

In 1436, a soothsayer warned James he would die if he spent the festive season at the Perth priory. However, this most unwelcome Christmas prescience was ignored. On 20 February 1437, after a night of merriment, James heard the sound of armed men outside. Realising immediately what was afoot, he ordered that the doors be locked – but the bolts had been removed. The King pulled up the wooden flooring and dropped down into the room below. At one time there had been an opening from there to the garden but James himself had had it sealed to prevent his tennis balls bouncing through it. It looked like game, set and match for the assassins but they had one volley yet to win before they could leap over the net. As they pushed at the door above, Kate Douglas, one of the queen's ladies in waiting, thrust her arm into the metal brackets which once housed the bolts. They had to break the door – and her arm – to get in. Finding the King in the room below, they leaped down, bristling with weapons.

James fought them off bravely but eventually was felled. He asked for a confessor but was told, 'No confessor shalt thou have but this sword.' And then he was stabbed, not just once but many times, the killer leaving the mangled body where it lay.

Although the Queen had been wounded, the assassins spared her life. They lived to regret such gallantry. The vengeful widow had them tracked down one by one and brutally executed. Among them was the Earl of Atholl, who over a three-day period endured the following: he was hoisted above the ground by the ankles then dropped suddenly to dislocate the joints; a red-hot crown was placed on his head to sear the flesh; he was then laid out on a rack, his heart and intestines cut from his body and burnt on a fire. Finally, his head was chopped off and his body quartered, with one of the pieces sent to Perth. I don't think he survived. His grandson Robert Graham got off comparatively lightly. He only had his right hand nailed to a gallows, then he was stabbed with red hot irons on various parts of his body (including his genitals) before being beheaded and quartered. On the corner of Charlotte Street and Blackfriars Street there is a plaque commemorating the assassination and also the battle of North Inch.

One of the oldest buildings in Perth is St John's Kirk, on St John's Street, although it has been altered over the years. Dating back to the thirteenth century, the area around the church, now built over, was once the burial ground. It was my interest in a sermon John Knox gave on 11 May 1559 that brought me here. The fiery reformer was so inspiring as he railed against idolatry that the congregation rioted. They attacked priests, and destroyed fittings and ornaments before moving on to the town's monasteries at Blackfriars and Greyfriars, stripping them of all ornamentation, demolishing statues and generally making pests of themselves. When Queen Mary of Guise set out with an army to punish the rioters, Knox and his supporters formed the 'Army of the Congregation' and prepared for war by all but destroying St Andrew's Cathedral and taking over the castle. Later, they took Edinburgh and forced the Queen back to Dunbar where she waited until reinforcements arrived from France. This then brought the English into the fray and Elizabeth sent first a fleet to Leith and later, when a formal treaty was signed between the reformers and her ministers, an army. When Mary died of dropsy in Edinburgh Castle, John Knox rejoiced, and the English and French got round the table and made peace. And to think all this started with one

bigoted man telling a crowd that to worship graven images was a sin.

In 1650, when the Scots accepted Charles II after he had decided to embrace the Covenant, the King spent many long, tedious hours in this church feigning interest in the incessant sermonising. After that, it may have come as a relief to be chased out of the country by Cromwell. His descendent, Charles Edward Stuart, also came here in 1745 and listened to a long, rambling sermon.

South Street, where the County Buildings now stand, was the site of Gowrie House, the setting for one of Scotland's most enduring – and perhaps least known – mysteries. It involves an intelligent (some may say cunning) but paranoid king, a mysterious stranger and a pot of gold. But to tell this tale of intrigue and murder, I must go back a few years in the life of young James VI.

James came to the monarchy at the age of 13 months while his mum, Mary, was imprisoned on Loch Leven. Not for the first time, the country was ruled by regents until the young king was of an age to take the day-to-day decisions of a Scottish monarch (for example who to execute, who to betray, who to forgive). During these years, James received the strong education that would ultimately lead to him being dubbed 'the wisest fool in Christendom', but he had few real friends, until 1579 when he met the dashing Esmé Stewart, Seigneur d'Aubigny. Then 37 years old, and a distant relation, Stewart was idolised by the impressionable teenage Jamie, who showered titles on the older man, including the Dukedom of Lennox. Another Stewart (James of Ochiltree) returned from fighting abroad and formed the third point in a chummy triangle, becoming the Earl of Arran. Through manipulation of the young lad, these two conspired with other nobles to have the former Regent Morton brought to trial and executed for his part in the murder of Jamie's father, Lord Darnley, all those years before. But if the two Stewarts thought they had their legs firmly under the royal table they were wrong. For Jamie's ministers, although glad to see the back of Morton, trusted them the way a fat man trusts a two-legged stool. The advisors felt the men exercised far too much influence on the young boy, especially in matters of religion. Scotland was still in the throes of the Reformation and even though the two men and the young King signed declarations condemning Roman Catholicism, the merest whiff of a Papal plot in the royal household was enough to have government ministers reaching for the rope.

It was decided that, for the good of the throne, the country and the church (although not necessarily in that order), the lad would have to be removed from their pernicious influence. So on 22 August 1582, the Earls of Gowrie, Glencairn and Mar snatched young James as he returned to Perth from a hunting trip in Atholl, in an abduction that became known as the 'Ruthven Raid'. He was taken to Ruthven Castle (which is just outside Perth on the A85 Crieff road, but is now known as Huntingtower) where he was kept in luxurious captivity for ten months. Patrick Ruthven, who had only recently been made Lord Gowrie, had a connection with James that extended as far as the womb, for he was one of the bloody earls who butchered David Rizzio in Holyrood. (He was also Mary's jailor while she was held in Loch Leven Castle but he lost the job, I was told, because he couldn't keep his codpiece fastened while around her.)

On arrival at Ruthven Castle, James burst into tears, which failed to move the rough men who looked down on him. 'Better bairns weep than bearded men,' the distraught teenager was told. The keeper of Huntingtower Castle told me that their intention was to 'make a man' of James and while he was held in the castle the earls' growing power forced both Lennox and Arran to make themselves scarce.

However, it was the conspirators' turn to scarper when James finally managed to break free and, backed by Huntly and Atholl, took back his throne. Only Gowrie refused to run scared. James showed a certain generosity of spirit after the abduction, pardoning all involved, but then in 1584 Gowrie found himself implicated in a new plot against the Crown and ended up losing his head. His lands and title eventually fell to his oldest son James and then, when he died aged 14, to John Ruthven. It was through Ruthven and his brother Alexander that James *may* have had his final revenge against the Ruthven family . . .

In 1600, James was in the process of trying to ensure his place on the throne of England. Old Queen Bess was ill but refused to name him officially as her successor – even though unofficially it seemed like a certainty. At home, meanwhile, he was in the middle of a struggle with the Kirk over the introduction of a form of episcopacy – a Stuart

obsession that would eventually cause their downfall. On 5 August, he was at Falkland Palace in the east, planning a stag hunt. Just as he was about to ride out, Alexander Ruthven arrived to tell him a curious tale. A dark stranger had appeared in Perth bearing a pot of gold. They had arrested the man and held him captive in Gowrie House, the townhouse of his brother, the Earl. The man, it was suggested, might be a papist agent sent to buy support for a new plot against the throne. The idea was to liberate the gold from the man and present it to the King. James weighed up his choices: ride out into the countryside and slaughter a few stags, or go to Perth and swell his personal treasury? For a king who seldom had much cash the choice was simple, so he headed off westwards to Perth. In woods around Falkland, the stags breathed an audible sigh of relief.

John Ruthven, Earl of Gowrie, met the King and his followers near Perth and rode with them back to his house. After a quick bite to eat – for the King did not believe in stealing another man's gold on an empty stomach – Gowrie led James to the room where the man was supposedly being kept. Somehow, the King had become separated from his bodyguards, who were now wandering about the streets looking for him. What happened in that room forms the core of the mystery.

According to James, the door was locked behind him and he turned to find not an old man hiding a pot of gold, but a younger man displaying a drawn dagger. Alexander Ruthven told him to prepare to meet his maker. It was well-known that James could not stand the sight of a drawn sword, let alone blood (and especially his own) so in a panic he leaped to a window and shouted, 'Treason! I am slain!' Clearly, he was not yet slain but the nobles below rushed up the stairs, forcing all the various locked doors open, and burst into the room. The two Ruthven brothers were killed during the subsequent swordplay and the King emerged without a scratch, thanking God for preserving him from such a peril.

On the face of it, the Gowrie Conspiracy was a plot against the life of the King, conceived by a family who had long opposed the Stuart will. The problem with the story is that it was the 'authorised King James edition' – and he didn't come out with it until one month after the killings. Few people actually believed it, not the least the Church, and several ministers across the land refused to read the official account from the pulpit – even under royal command. According to James, the tall, dark man in the townhouse was Andrew Henderson, a Gowrie servant, but he was actually small and ruddy-faced. Henderson did admit being there but was he executed for his part in the assassination attempt? No – he was released and granted a king's pension. And if murder was on the minds of the Ruthven brothers, why did they invite James *and* his armed retainers? And why did they hesitate when James entered the room, giving him enough time to reach the window and cry out? Why did they wait until his men had fought their way up to the locked room without even bruising him, let alone finishing him off?

There have been suspicions that James plotted the whole thing. He feared the Ruthven ambition and possible vengeance – he had, after all, executed their father. He also owed them money and a murder or two was cheaper than meeting his financial obligations.

But there is another theory, and it's one based on suspicions over James's sexuality. There have been theories long-held that he was what modern tabloids might once have called a 'ballet-loving bachelor'. The Ruthven men were young, virile and handsome and James may possibly have taken a fancy to one, or both. A sexual advance might have been made, rejected and the assassination story invented to cover it all up. But these theories about James's leanings are only conjecture.

Although they were dead the Ruthven brothers' bodies were taken to Edinburgh where they were indicted for high treason. The title of the 'Earldom of Gowrie' was stripped from the family, their lands were forfeited – even the name Ruthven was abolished and the castle was renamed. The dead men's bodies were hanged, drawn and quartered, with parts of the corpses returned to Perth for public display.

THIRTY-THREE
Pounding Stirling

On the death of Queen Anne, James Stuart, the Old Pretender, was given the opportunity to have his kingdom returned to his family as long as he renounced Roman Catholicism. He clearly could not do so in good conscience and so the British throne went instead to George of Hanover, the 'wee German Lairdie' as he became known in Scotland. John Erskine, Earl of Mar, raised the Stuart standard in Aberdeenshire on 6 September 1715, having suffered a dramatic conversion to Jacobitism when the newly crowned George I sacked him as Secretary of State for Scotland. Although his forces managed to occupy both Inverness and Perth, the hoped-for French aid never came. The rebellion was short-lived and marked in Scotland by only one battle, such as it was. To reach the memorial marking the conflict, I left Huntingtower for the A9. Some distance on towards Stirling I turned right at the sign for Sheriffmuir and followed a narrow country road that skirted the foot of the Ochil Hills, finally turning right at a sign for Dunblane before coming upon the large monument at the roadside.

It was on the marshy, frost-covered land around here on 13 November 1715 that Mar's Highlanders met government troops under the Earl of Argyll, outnumbering them by two to one. The subsequent fight was bloody but unresolved. As the Scottish ballad tells us,

> A battle there was that I saw man,
> And we ran and they ran
> And they ran and we ran
> And we ran and they ran awa', man!

Mar retreated to Perth and Argyll claimed victory. James Edward

Stuart landed in Scotland just before Christmas but by then it was clear there would be no further uprising, no hope of regaining the throne. After six weeks – during which he ordered that the countryside be burned to deprive Argyll's advancing troops of supplies – the Old Pretender quietly slipped away again, never to return. To his credit, he ordered that any money left after his troops had been paid should be used to compensate those people who had suffered during his scorched earth policy. The next Stuart to land in Scotland would be his son, Charles Edward.

The monument here was erected in memory of the members of the Clan MacCrae, who fell almost to a man while defending the Royal House of Stuart.

Leaving Sheriffmuir, I followed the road through Dunblane and back onto the A9. I took the road south and was treated to what for my money is the best view of Stirling Castle. The motorway slid over the crest of a hill and spread out below me was the Stirling plain with the castle perched on its rock to the left, the town trailing away behind it. This was the jewel in the castle chain, and has been described as being 'like a huge brooch, clasping Highlands and Lowlands together'. As such it was strategically important. Thousands of men have died over the centuries in defending the place, or trying to take it. Later I was to visit the site of the most famous of all the battles in this part of Scotland, but for now I planned to spend some time in the castle itself.

There is a large car park at the top of the wynd and from here you can explore not just the castle but also the streets of the old town leading up to it. The attractions on this steep hill include Stirling's old town jail, built in 1847 after a visiting judge poked his nose into the overcrowded cell at the tollbooth and announced that it was not fit for human habitation. The building is now a museum and in it the visitor can see what conditions were like in a Victorian jail. Not far away is the Mercat Cross, topped by the statue of a unicorn known as the 'Puggy'. This was the scene of a riot in December 1706 when locals protested over the union with England, angry over the parcel of rogues who had sold out Scotland's independence for a handful of gold.

And so to the castle itself. For many years this was an active military base but it is now in the keeping of the National Trust. On the esplanade stands a magnificent (if slightly rotund) statue of Robert the Bruce looking nobly in the direction of his greatest victory at Bannockburn. After the battle he began to tear the castle apart to prevent it ever being used again. Later kings rebuilt it – for which the tourist industry is most grateful. Across the valley the Wallace Monument exclaims against the sky from its vantage point on wooded Abbey Craig. And between the memorials to the two heroes is the site of the Battle of Stirling Bridge, where Wallace and Andrew De Moray took on the might of Edward I, and won.

Although other battles were fought around the castle, and it was besieged many times (the gatehouse still shows the marks of cannonballs), it has seen other dark doings too. James I had nobles beheaded here as part of his campaign to curb their power. Whereas his son dispensed with the services of an executioner and got in some hands-on action himself.

The object of his displeasure was William, eighth Earl of Douglas. Traditionally, his murder is said to have taken place in what is known as the Old King's Building but actually the building did not exist in 1452. According to the story, James II was suspicious of the power gathered by the Douglas family and invited William, head of the family, for a wee chat. He even provided a letter of safe conduct. After a pleasant dinner, the King tried to dissuade William from amassing any further power and from plotting against the throne. The Earl refused and the enraged King stabbed him twice while one of his courtiers, Sir Patrick Grey, waded in with an axe. The Earl's body was then tipped from a window. Naturally, William's kinfolk were not very chuffed with the way their leader had been treated, especially as his safety had been guaranteed by the King. They laid siege to the castle, pinned the safe conduct letter to the tail of the oldest, smelliest horse they could find and dragged it through the muddy streets.

It was in the castle chapel that James IV confessed to his part in the assassination of his father. James III had angered the nobles, just as his grandfather had done, and they rose against him, getting his son to support them. They did not like the way the elder James played

DEVIL'S GALLOP 163

favourites with men they regarded as beneath them (artisans and masons) and so after hanging most of them in front of the King, they launched a rebellion. At Sauchieburn, not far from the site of Bruce's victory at Bannockburn, the two sides clashed. But the King's nerve deserted him. He had never been one for a fight, and he galloped off, falling off his horse near a mill. He was taken in by the miller and his wife to whom he said, 'I was your King this morning.'

James then said he needed a priest to whom he could confess his sins. Eventually, a holy man appeared and leaned over the King, who promptly felt a bit deflated. This could have been due to his defeat in battle, or even the wind being knocked out of him in his fall. Or it could have been because the so-called priest was in the process of letting the air out of him with the point of a dagger. Five times the bogus cleric stabbed him around the heart – and Scotland had a new king, young James, then 19 years of age, who is said to have worn an iron belt around his waist until he died as a symbol of his remorse over his own part in the regicide.

Despite his means of obtaining the crown, he proved to be an able king. He strengthened the army, tried to create a navy, endeared himself to his people and embarked on a regime of palace-building the like of which had never been seen before, including a great deal of work at Stirling. The Great Hall was part of his handiwork, and when it was recently restored it caused something of a storm with its lime-washed walls standing out against the blackened stone of the surrounding buildings. However, this is how the whole castle would have looked at one time. He built magnificent palaces at Holyrood, Edinburgh, Falkland and Linlithgow and who knows what else he might have achieved had he not perished with the flower of Scottish nobility at the bloodbath that was Flodden.

But as I left Stirling it was not defeats I had in mind but perhaps the greatest victory over the richer, more powerful nation to the south that Scotland has ever had. Its very name has come to represent the country's long-running struggle for freedom, and it's the place where Robert the Bruce turned from a mildly successful, politically astute king to a freedom-loving, fully fledged, honest-to-goodness, slap-his-face-on-a-t-shirt hero.

THIRTY-FOUR

Now is the Day, now is the Hour

There are three battles that evoke strong feelings in historically-minded Scots. Culloden is one. For the second it's a coin toss between Flodden and Stirling Bridge. But the third is most definitely Bannockburn.

Edward Longshanks died on 7 July 1307. He died as he had lived, hammering away at the Scots, determined to bring his one-time ally Robert the Bruce under his thumb. But as he rode north at the head of yet another invading army, his old body betrayed him and at Burgh-on-Sands on the south coast of the Solway, he died. Even in death, though, Longshanks wanted to spit defiance at the rebellious Scots. His son, soon to be Edward II, was told to melt the flesh from his bones and carry the tall skeleton northwards at the head of the army. But young Edward ignored his father's last wishes and had the body removed to Westminster Abbey – although his brain and entrails were buried amid great pomp in Holm Cultram Abbey, south of Carlisle.

Edward II was not the tactician or the warrior his father had been and you wonder what might have happened at Bannockburn if Longshanks had lived. After his old enemy's death, Bruce continued the guerrilla campaign that had made him such a thorn in England's flesh. He took the castles that were in English hands, destroying them so they could not be used to subjugate Scotland again. By 1313, his brother Edward, who was as belligerent as he, was besieging Stirling Castle, then in the English hands of Sir Philip de Mowbray. It was slow going. Edward Bruce was becoming more impatient as days turned to weeks and then months. Inside the impregnable fortress, the English knew that supplies were far from infinite. So a deal was made between the two commanders – if reinforcements did not arrive from England within one year of the Feast of St John the Baptist on 24 June, then the castle would be surrendered into Scottish hands.

Neither Bruce nor Edward II liked this arrangement when they heard it. Bruce knew this would force the English to come north mob-handed. Edward, on the other hand, was insulted that the Scots could even think that he would allow such a jewel simply to be handed over – even under the terms of a gentleman's agreement. So Edward raised an army, and sent messengers out across Europe to bring back his best, most battle-hardened knights; and the great juggernaut of the English army came to Scotland again. With one day to go before the deadline, they met the Scots at Bannockburn, south of Stirling.

To find what is deemed to be the site of the battle (and my last port of call on this trip) I followed the signs from the centre of Stirling. There is a heritage centre at the battleground, complete with exhibition and a film show. The monument itself is a large concrete rotunda that is, to be honest, a bit of an eyesore. A stone cairn inside this commemorates the battle, quoting the Declaration of Arbroath. It was apparently erected near the spot where the Bruce raised his standard. However the focal point for most of the cameras is the huge statue of Robert the Bruce on horseback, battle-axe at the ready.

There is some doubt as to where the hostilities actually raged but until firm evidence is found to locate it elsewhere, this site will have to do. Unfortunately, like other sites of historic interest, housing is encroaching the fringes.

The battle was fought over two days: the Sunday and Monday. The English wanted to fight on their terms; on a flat field that gave them the chance to employ the medieval tank – the cavalry. But their horses would have to cross a narrow gorge to reach the Scottish emplacements. Their arrogance saw them more or less dismiss the effectiveness of the Scottish schiltrons (blocks of spearmen grouped together with their spear points facing outwards like the spikes on a hedgehog). The Scots had used this tactic before with varying degrees of success but Bruce had been training his men day and night for months and had introduced a new surprise – these schiltrons could move as one man.

Bruce himself drew first blood. He was in front of his army, mounted on a garron (a small horse without armour). An English knight, Sir Henry de Bohun, recognised the circle of gold on the

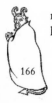

King's helmet and decided to make a name for himself. Lowering his visor, he couched his lance and spurred his great war-horse forward. Bruce saw the charge and realised he was in a vulnerable position.

He was on a small, light pony. He was alone. And he only had a battle-axe for a weapon. This did not look good.

Nonetheless, he stood his ground and waited. He continued to wait, keeping his little pony still, as de Bohun galloped across the ground, the point of his lance steadily trained on Bruce. Then, just as the Englishman drew level, Bruce jerked the reins to one side, and got out of the way of the lumbering charge. Raising himself up on his stirrups, he brought his axe crashing down into the knight's helmet, slicing through metal and bone.

Whether this close encounter spurred Bruce's men on to victory is hard to say, for not all would have seen it. Bruce, though, was phlegmatic about it all. Apparently all he had to say afterwards was something along the lines of, 'That bastard broke my axe.' But once again he had shown that the English were not superhuman, and that they could be beaten – and by the end of the following day, beaten they were. The schiltrons held against repeated cavalry charges, while the marshy ground and the caltrops (metal spikes strewn on the ground to injure horses) took their toll. English archers firing into the fray, cutting down many of their own men did not help matters for them. At one point, though, Edward was delighted to see the Scots kneeling before him. He thought they were begging him for mercy until it was pointed out to him that in fact they were kneeling before the Breacbannoch, a silver casket carrying the bones of either St Andrew or St Columba.

But in the end the battle was decided by the infantry pushing and hacking at each other on the field. For a time it seemed the conflict could go either way until slowly the English ranks began to break and Edward's generals convinced him all was lost. They tried to reach the safety of the castle but were refused entry, so Edward and his retinue, comprising a large body of heavily armed men, had to skirt around the Scottish forces and head south. Meanwhile his troops, seeing him retreat, lost heart and also began to flee, pursued by Scottish troops and the 'small folk' – non-combatants who nevertheless wanted to be in at the kill. The English were slaughtered as they ran, their bodies choking streams and lying in gory beds on the grass. Between three and four thousand would-be invaders died in those two days, including many of Edward's best knights. Bruce, on the other hand, lost around 400 men.

With this victory, the Scots believed they had won their freedom. There were, as we know, further struggles ahead – with Edward, Henry, and Elizabeth, up until the point that the greed of a Stuart king (James VI), who hungered for the power and riches of the Crown of England, saw that freedom subjugated once again. The Jacobites carried its torch for a time but their cause was a doomed one which, as we know, led the country into the kind of oppression that was the stuff Longshank's dreams were made of. Between Cumberland's dramatic steps to ensure the Jacobites never rebelled again and the Clearances of the nineteenth century, the Highland way of life changed. Clansmen still fought, not for Chief or King across the water, but for Empire. They fought and they died in Canada, the Americas, Africa, Asia and Europe. They fought proudly, for the spirits of Bannockburn and Stirling Bridge and even Culloden still burned brightly. But in many cases, all they were doing was continuing what Cumberland's Redcoats started after 1746 – helping to stamp out cultures that were simply in the way of someone else's idea of progress.

And with that depressing thought, I headed back to Glasgow.

DEVIL'S GALLOP

APPIN WAY

DUMBARTON ROCK – GLEN
FRUIN – LOCH LOMOND –
DALRIGH – ACHALLADER
CASTLE – GLENCOE –
BALLACHULISH – APPIN –
PORTNACOISH – PASS OF
BRANDER – LOCH DOCHART –
LOCH LUBHAIR –
BALQUHIDDER – ABERFOYLE –
LAKE OF MENTEITH

THIRTY-FIVE
The High Road

Loch Lomond and the Trossachs are the lungs of Glasgow. It is this mountainous area that many city dwellers go to to escape the concrete bonds of the streets and just breathe. If they are of an active disposition, there is so much to do. Or else visitors can just drink in the scenery which is okay if all you want is perfection. Even when the weather glowers (and remember, Scotland has the most ill-tempered climate in Britain) the landscape here is something to see. Mist crowds around the tops of the hills, turning what is on a clear day a serene mountain view into something much more mysterious. It is easy to believe dark things can happen here when the cold waters of the loch turn grey and the streams bleed out of the hillside like open wounds.

I left Glasgow via the Great Western Road, one of the two great arterial routes west. Once beyond the city limits the speed restrictions eased until I hit Dumbarton – and my first stop. Way back in the mists of time, Dumbarton was the ancient capital of Strathclyde. The Dumbarton of those far-off days was not the bustling big town we see today. The focal point was the lump of rock extending into the river known as 'Alt-cluaithe', or 'Rock of the Clyde'. Later it would become known as 'Dun Breatann', or 'the fortress of the Britons', from which its modern name is derived. To reach the rock, I simply followed the signs. I would not have such luxuries later on this trip.

Although the best way to see it is from across the River Clyde, Dumbarton Rock is hugely impressive. The climb to the top is a bit of a haul, especially when you are as unfit as I am, but it is worth it, offering views up-river to the Clyde Firth, down-river to the city, across to Ayrshire and up the country to Loch Lomond and the Highlands. They say it was the longest-occupied fortress in the country, although the soldiers are long gone now. In its time it has been a royal court, a prison, a frontier fort and a prisoner of war camp. According to legend, not only did Merlin visit the place, but William Wallace was also imprisoned behind the walls. No one can say for certain if the first story is true but my guide book assured me that the second one is almost certainly not – despite the presence of a 'Wallace Tower' and the fact that Sir John Menteith, the noble who betrayed Wallace in 1305, was made governor of Dumbarton by Longshanks.

Dumbarton was used many times as an embarkation point for France. David II fled from here to the security of the auld allies after his army was defeated by the invading English at Halidon Hill in 1333. James I's young daughter Margaret left Scotland from here to marry the French Dauphin. She died, aged 20, an unhappy wife, longing to see her native land once again. And in 1548, another Scottish princess, Mary, later to become Queen of Scots, also sailed from here to marry a Dauphin. She was spirited away to France after the disastrous Rough Wooing defeat at Pinkiecleugh.

Being a fortress, Dumbarton Rock has seen many violent acts. In 870 the Vikings came here for a spot of pillaging. They laid siege, starved out the populace then carried off the survivors and what riches they could find to their headquarters in Ireland. Almost 150 years later, Duncan (of Macbeth fame) was made King of Strathclyde by his father. He retained this title until 1034 when he became King of Scots and the region became part of the greater kingdom. Siege engines were back here again in 1489, after James III got the point in Perth (see Rebel March), and his son arrived to flush out some rebellious nobles. A huge cannon known as Mons Meg was used to batter the garrison into submission. In 1513, after James IV's death at Flodden, power-hungry nobles were once again fighting over Dumbarton. Lord Erskine had taken the rock and castle in the name of Mary of Guise, but followers of the Regent Earl of Arran retook it one year later by digging a tunnel under the north gate. In 1570, a siege ordered here by the Regent Moray (after Mary was taken into captivity in England) only ended when Moray himself was killed in Linlithgow.

However the most famous military action here came in 1571 when Lord Fleming was loyally holding the castle in the name of his imprisoned Queen Mary. Captain Thomas Crawford of Jordanhill led his men up the eastern side of the rock using ladders and ropes brought from Glasgow by an overnight march. A thick mist helped cover their progress until they pulled themselves over the top of the wall and surprised the part of the garrison known as 'the Beak', managing to turn the artillery there on the rest of the castle.

Over the centuries, the rock has played host to many noble and ignoble prisoners, including Bad Lord Soules who was brought here for his part in a plot against Robert the Bruce. Covenanters and Jacobites also found themselves sent here by vengeful governments and during the Napoleonic Wars, French POWs too enjoyed the brisk river air here.

Much of what we see now was developed by General Wade. The oldest part of the fortress is the fourteenth-century portcullis arch, which crosses the stairs leading up a chasm between the rocks to the summit.

Having clambered all over Dumbarton Rock, enjoyed the view and sat for a moment to pacify my protesting muscles, I left the town, and followed signs for Loch Lomond. I contemplated making a pilgrimage to Cardross, where Robert the Bruce died, but as there is nothing left of his great manor I decided against it. Instead, I made my way back to the A82, a fine wide road that took me speedily to the southernmost tip of the loch and here I had the first hint of the scenic splendours to come. The A82 travels up the west side of the loch on its way north, where four valleys bisect the hills to the west towards Loch Long (which despite its name is not as long as Lomond). I decided to take the B831 to find Glen Fruin, which was to be the first site on my trip concerned with the fearsome Clan MacGregor. It was a bloody event here that helped lead to their very name being banned by a genocidal royal decree that placed a price, literally, on any MacGregor head.

This band of reiving ruffians took their name from Grogar, son of King Alpin – hence their clan motto: 'Royal is my race.' They were fierce, proud and, like many other Highland clans, not averse to a touch of larceny here and there when the notion took them – and the notion took them more often than not. This disrespect for other

DEVIL'S GALLOP

people's property meant they were not well-liked by their neighbours, be they Campbell, MacDonald or Colquhoun. However, it was while accepting the Earl of Argyll's shilling that they took the final step towards their downfall.

The Campbell chief, Archibald Campbell of Argyll, at that time was eyeing the lands of Colquhoun of Luss from his stronghold in Inveraray and he invited the MacGregors to help him add it to his own property. Although they hated the Campbells, the MacGregors readily agreed, for their clan had suffered under policies promoted by the Crown (in which a landlord was held responsible for the actions of his tenants). As the MacGregors were a thorn in so many sides no one wished to see them on their lands. So in 1603, when Argyll offered them the job of harrying the Colquhouns, they must have thought that having the Campbell chief on their side for once would be no bad thing. They descended on the lands around Luss, carried off what cattle they could find and killed what men got in their way. Colquhoun knew that Argyll was behind the raid but there was no way he was going to accuse him. Argyll was, after all, Justice General of Scotland and one of the King's favourites. So Colquhoun blamed the MacGregors completely, demanding from James I and VI a letter of 'Fire and Sword' against them.

However, Alasdair of Glenstrae, the MacGregor chieftain, believed that the best form of defence was attack, so he gathered his stongest men, as well as some MacDonalds, Campbells and Camerons, and struck out towards Luss again. It was at Strone in Glen Fruin that he and his 400 men clashed with a combined Colquhoun and Buchanan force that was double their number. The MacGregor men were hardened fighters, used to wielding a claymore in self-defence or while relieving enemies of their goods. The home side was made up of farmers and townspeople from Dumbarton. In the end, the topography of the glen worked against the defenders and the MacGregors left 200 of them dead – at the cost of only two of their own men. Among the fallen, according to Colquhoun claims, was a group of young students who had somehow become caught up in the thick of the fighting. According to one story, they took refuge in a barn that was then set alight. But according to another version, a MacDonald slit their throats. When he was asked what had happened to them, the man held out his dirk and said, 'Ask that and God help me!' It took six years for the man to be tracked down and executed for his murderous act.

Colquhoun sent widows with the bloody shirts of their dead husbands hung on spear points to the King and again demanded vengeance. James was notoriously squeamish at the sight of blood – even when it was not his own, and was none too pleased with the rout of the force he had sanctioned to punish the MacGregors. In his rage he ordered that an Act be passed to outlaw the entire clan. From then on, it was legal to 'extirpat Clan Gregor and ruit out their posterities and their name'. This meant that anyone bearing the name MacGregor was fair game. They could be killed and a reward claimed on their head. What lands they had were taken from them and the clan was dispersed, forced even further into the Highland wilderness, where they turned more and more to raiding and robbery, earning themselves the name 'Children of the Mist' for the speed with which they struck and disappeared.

MacGregors to this day tell a different story – they saw that the grieving widows Colquhoun sent to Stirling were in fact ladies of the night, specially hired to weep and wail, and that the bloody shirts were actually stained with sheep's blood.

Returning to the A82, I made my way north again, turning off only when I found the signs leading to Luss, a nice little village which is as good a place as any to view the loch. (It is also where external scenes for the soap opera *High Road* are filmed, if that sort of thing is to your viewing taste.) In the sixth century an Irish prince called Kessog came here and built a monastery on one of the islands just off the shore. He was murdered, apparently, near Bandry Bay, just outside Luss, in 530 AD. He was later sanctified and the small church in the village is named after him.

The church is well worth a look, although on the day I visited for this tour, the graveyard looked as if it had been recently visited by a particularly vicious whirlwind. Gravestones had been uprooted and were lying face down in the grass or propped up against the church wall. But still standing were the memorials to members of the Colquhoun family, as well as a stone near the front door of the church

erected in memory of James, the 11th baronet, and some friends who lost their lives in a boating accident on the loch.

The famous song about taking the high road to Loch Lomond has its roots in the tale of a young Jacobite held prisoner in London prior to his execution. He tells his lover that she must take the high road back to their beloved loch while he takes 'the low road' after his death.

Many of the loch's 30 islands have played a vital role in local history. Inchcailleach was a MacGregor burial isle. Eilean Inchvow was a stronghold of the MacFarlanes. Robert the Bruce is said to have ordered that Inchlonaig be seeded with yew trees to provide the raw materials for the longbows that would help in the struggle with the English and the MacGregors proved that if you gave them an Inch they'd take everything for miles, by using Inchmurrin as a staging post during a very curious raid. Their lands were on the other side of the loch, around Glen Arklet, and they realised that government troops could surprise them by sailing across, so they decided to steal as many boats as they could. They rowed across to Inchmurrin and waited until night fell before travelling to the western shore and taking what boats they could back to the island. They waited for a day and then took their curious little fleet back to the other side. But the government had horses tow a fleet of gunboats up the River Leven and they bombarded the MacGregor hideout anyway. Inchmurrin itself was later used as an asylum for lunatics and drunkards.

The loch was also the scene of another curious naval action, this time involving the Viking troops of King Haakon in 1263. The rich lands along the lochside attracted the Norse raiders and the King sent 60 ships up Loch Long to Arrochar, where they were beached and dragged overland to Tarbet (it's actually not that great a feat, for it's only a distance of about two miles). The ships were then relaunched and the Norsemen proceeded to raid the lands of Lennox, putting the islands to the flame, raping, pillaging and no doubt laughing heartily in the manner of Ernest Borgnine and Kirk Douglas.

I made my way back to the A82 to continue my journey north. I stayed on the lochside road, admiring the incredible scenery, turning for Crianlarich at Tarbet. The road narrows here but still clings tenaciously to the side of the loch until it comes to the popular 'Poachers Inn' where it leaves the water behind. I was now in Glen

Falloch, which starts off wooded, peaceful and gentle but becomes bleak, rocky and steep further on. It was here centuries ago that three men came from the north to find one Duncan Dhu with whom they had some murderous business. They met a man hacking at the trunk of a great tree and they asked where they could find Duncan – and what he looked like, for although they meant to settle an old score, they had never actually met him. The man said he would take them to him if they would first help him split the tree. They agreed and as they positioned themselves against the trunk, the man swiftly knocked away the wedge that held it steady, trapping them underneath. For this man, of course, was Duncan Dhu – and with his would-be assassins thus incapacitated he was able to despatch them with ease, using his axe.

THIRTY-SIX
The King's Field

Crianlarich acts as a kind of gateway to the north, for the fault line that divides Highland from Lowland runs not far from here. The West Highland Railway also steams through here, while the West Highland Way, a favourite among walkers and charity fund-raisers, steps close by on its way to further scenic splendours in the north. I remained on the A82, following signs for Tyndrum, but a few miles out of Crianlarich I made another stop to look for the site of one of Robert the Bruce's lesser known battles. This time he was not fighting the English but fellow Scots. And this time he lost.

A sign for Dalrigh was the first hint that the battleground was nearby. I turned left off the road and found a car park. This surprised me because this battle site was not marked on any of the maps I had with me, and yet here I was presented not only with a car park, but also with pathways. There was, however, nothing to tell me in which direction to walk. I knew, though, that the battle was fought near a river, so I set off towards it. Sure enough, I had not walked far along the riverbank (turning right at a blocked bridge) when I found a stone bench with the legend 'BATTLE OF DALRIGH 1306' etched on the top. I took a variety of photographs from every angle – for I am nothing if not cavalier with film – and then sat on the bench to reflect on the events surrounding the battle, which was really little more than a skirmish.

Bruce had been crowned King in March at Scone. To say this vexed Edward Longshanks is to put it mildly. The big man threw a severe strop and appointed his cousin Aymer De Valance as his lieutenant, sending him north to unfurl the dragon banner that signified that no quarter would be given. Bruce soon found out that you didn't take liberties with Valance when he was ambushed near Perth and forced to flee westwards. He eventually found himself here, in Strathfillan, where he decided to visit the shrine at the priory of St Fillan for a quick prayer. Bruce thought highly of this saint (or at least of the bones of the man's left arm which were kept in a reliquary at the priory). John MacDougall of Lorne, whose lands lay over the hills to the west, heard the king was nearby. He was related on his mother's side to the Red Comyn, who Bruce had attacked (and possibly killed) in a church in Dumfries, and he decided this was as good a chance as any for payback. Bruce's small party met them here but were soon on the run from MacDougall's larger force. Bruce, though, fought like a lion, his great battle axe slicing down anyone within range. According to legend, three MacDougalls (some say it was the chief and two sons) tried to drag him from his horse but Bruce killed all three. The last man to succumb to the axe grabbed the King's plaid as he fell, pulling off the crystal and pearl clasp. This item, known as the 'Brooch of Lorne', has been handed down from generation to generation among the chiefs of the MacDougalls. The field where this all took place is behind the bench monument. Since that day it has been known as Dalrigh, or 'King's Field', in memory of the skirmish.

The King, bitter over his defeat first by the English and then by his own countrymen, headed west into the hills, angrily throwing his sword into the waters of Lochan nan Arm. (The sword is still there, it is said.) But he would have his revenge on the MacDougalls.

St Fillan, whom the priory here is named after, was the son of an Irish princess and one of the first missionaries to come to the mainland from Iona, after Columba. He stayed for a time in Fife, where he developed something of a reputation for being able to translate the scriptures in the dark by using his glowing left hand as a candle. (This was either a divine gift or he had been working too close to a nuclear power station.)

What remains of the priory can be reached by following the path back beyond the closed-off bridge and crossing the A85 (be careful, the cars travel very fast on this stretch of road). A side road leads past some farm buildings at Auchtertyre and the ruins, such as they are, can be found near Kirkton Farm.

178   DEVIL'S GALLOP

Also near here is St Fillan's Pool, the site of some very strange medical treatment. Anyone afflicted with insanity (suffering from delusions, strange fits, or a tendency to buy CDs of accordion music) was bound hand and foot before being tossed into the icy waters here. If the patient bobbed to the surface having grabbed a large pebble from the bottom, then he or she was declared cured. The pebble was added to one of three cairns on the bank. A second stage of the cure could involve the bound patient lying out all night, dripping wet, on a slab in the priory. If by morning the person was freed from his or her bonds this was said to be thanks to the intervention of St Fillan and they were declared sane. If not, they were deemed to be as crazy as bedbugs, to use a medical term.

A few minutes further along the A85 is Tyndrum, where the road forks west towards Oban, and north towards Glencoe. I kept going north, with the well-trodden path of the West Highland Way marching along the hillside on the right, following the route of an old military road, and the railway line above it. The scenery here is truly stunning, with a deep valley separating the road from the steep-sided mountains. I was now in the Grampians and mist often hangs around the peaks (especially the pointed Beinn Dorain) shielding them from the eyes of passing motorists. I have often thought of making my way down into the valley but the only road I can see is marked 'STRICTLY PRIVATE' and my fear of some angry landowner armed with dogs, a shotgun and a solicitor's phone number has always kept me on the main road.

The road took me past the hotel at Bridge of Orchy and on until I reached the shores of Loch Tulla, where I turned right onto a small track marked 'ACHALLADER'. The road here was rough and rocky and the tyres of my car, more used to tarmac than off-road exploration, screamed in complaint. The track ended at a collection of farm buildings and the remains of a tower, the object of this particular diversion. It was built by Black Duncan Campbell, sometimes known as 'Duncan of the Seven Castles' because – wait for it – he had seven castles. He took these particular lands from the Fletcher family by trickery. He sent an English servant to pasture a horse in a corn field near to the Fletcher's house. The owners warned the man in Gaelic that he would be shot if he did not remove himself and his nag, but the man did not understand. So the Fletchers shot him. At that point, Black Duncan happened by, feigning concern over the murder. He told the Fletcher chief that his life and lands would be forfeit when the authorities heard of the deed, and urged him to leave for France. To protect the chief's family, Black Duncan offered to buy the lands from him (for nothing, naturally) but under the terms of the deal would return them to the Fletchers when the scandal had died down. The chief agreed – and of course never got his lands back.

Originally the tower had three storeys and a garret but during a Jacobite rebellion in 1689 it was burned down, allowed to deteriorate and now forms part of a byre. There was also a clan battle fought here, it is said, and cairns were built to mark the graves of the dead. However, I could find no trace of them, nor any notes about them on the Ordnance Survey map. I was told by a woman in the farmhouse that they were somewhere near the railway line, which runs along the side of the hill. But the only note of a cairn I could find was one dedicated to a shepherd girl called McNee who was caught up in a fight between MacDonald cattle thieves and angry Campbells. The girl was killed during the fighting and the cairn erected to mark the spot. And that is quite some distance into the hills.

In 1691 Iain Glas, Grey John Campbell, the first Earl of Breadalbane, invited the rebellious Highland leaders here to sign a treaty to end their struggle against King William. Breadalbane was described as 'cunning as a fox, wise as a serpent and slippery as an eel'. He brought fifteen thousand pounds with him to the meeting with which to tempt the chiefs – if he could not appeal to their sense of loyalty then at least he could excite their nose for a bargain. In the end, one of the only chiefs to hold out was McIain of Glencoe, and his refusal had disastrous consequences for him and his family.

I headed back to the A82, turned right over a metal bridge crossing the Water of Tulla, then climbed a steep hill to a lay-by and viewpoint which boasted a mobile snack bar and a cairn dedicated to those many hundreds of people who have died on Scotland's mountains during this century. This cairn also remembers Sir Hugh Munro, the man who charted the peaks over 3,000 feet that are now called 'Munros' after him. Each of the 750 stones here was brought from a different Munro and erected at this picturesque spot overlooking the Loch Tulla.

THIRTY-SEVEN

Glen of Weeping

Moving onwards, with the Black Mount rising on my left, I skirted the western edge of Rannoch Moor, a vast stretch of bleak and marshy peat covering about 20 miles. Readers of Robert Louis Stevenson's *Kidnapped* will know it well, for it was across its heathery desolation that the redcoats pursued Allan Breck and David Balfour. 'A wearier looking desert a man never saw,' wrote Stevenson but methinks the man was being a touch hard on it. Certainly, even now, there is no road across it but it is a fine sight, even when blanketed with mist and rain.

Soon the dark bulk of Buachaille Etive Mor, the 'Great Herdsman of Etive', was looming on my left, standing guard at the mouth of Glencoe, and the road seemed to narrow as the mountains crowded in on all sides. Surely anyone who can drive into Glencoe without feeling overawed is either kidding themselves or is so spiritually dead that nothing can touch them. Like Culloden, there is a dark spirit at work here, and there always seem to be shadows around. Jagged rocks rise steeply on either side of the road and the flanks of the hills, scarred with deep gouges that seem to have been made by some titanic creature, rise sharply to ragged peaks that disappear into wet mists. The feeling is that the glen is at the centre of a huge range of mountains all of its own, but the reality is that there are only three actual peaks – Buachaille Etive Mor (3,345 feet), Buachaille Etive Beag (3,129 feet) and Bidean nam Bian (3,766 feet), all to the south of the valley – and a ridge of rock to the north.

Just before I entered the Pass of Glencoe, my attention was caught by a large cairn on the right, opposite the track from Glen Etive. I stopped and examined it but there was nothing to explain what it was. Later, I asked at the visitors' centre and was told it was the site of a coffin trail. Highlanders believed that the dead would rest easily when buried with their kinfolk, so coffins were carried over certain roads to the deceased's place of birth. When the people of Etive brought coffins over the hill for burial in Glencoe or Ballachulish they stopped here and laid a rock on the cairn to give thanks for a safe journey. The cairn I saw was a (much-tidied-up) version of the original. The guide told me that when the Blackwater Dam was being constructed at the beginning of the twentieth century, Irish navvies made their way to the Kingshouse Hotel via the Devil's Staircase, a zig-zag path over the hills. Two of them were told there was a bottle of whisky hidden under this cairn and they spent all night dismantling it to find it. Those navvies were lucky to survive, for many of their colleagues were caught on the Devil's Staircase by ferocious snow storms, their bodies not found until the spring thaw.

The narrow pass eventually widens into an arable valley floor which is peppered with walkers making their way to hillside paths, and with the ubiquitous sheep, the four-footed Highlander. As I plunged deeper into the glen, I thought about the events here one snow-filled night in 1691. Like many another incidents in Scottish history, the full story of the Glencoe massacre is not as well known to Scots as it should be. Most know an atrocity was committed here – perhaps even that it was a blatant breach of the Highland laws of hospitality, but many believe the English were responsible. This was an example, however, of Scots' cruelty towards their own kind, albeit in the name of a Dutchman on an English throne.

The MacDonalds came to Glencoe after Robert the Bruce granted them the lands following his victory at the Pass of Brander (more on this later). Like the other clans (in particular the MacGregors) the MacDonalds were accomplished cattle thieves, who had perfected the trick of stealing cows from their neighbours and spiriting them away to hidden gullies and valleys in Glencoe. On one raid into Breadalbane, their swag bag was so full that they ruined many families – notably that of Captain Robert Campbell of Glenlyon, who was related by marriage to the Glencoe MacDonalds. Their larcenous behaviour reached such a pitch that they became known as 'The Gallows Herd'.

The MacDonalds were also Jacobites who had fought at Killicrankie for Bonnie Dundee against King William's forces. This battle ended in victory for the Jacobite cause but was in reality, with the death of Dundee, the beginning of the end for that particular dream (see Rebel March). Two years later, a magnanimous William offered all Highland rebel chiefs a pardon, as long as they declared their allegiance to him before 1691 was out. Certain bribes were offered at Achallader. The astute chiefs realised that for them the future was orange and they swore their oath. By the end of the year only MacIain of Glencoe was hesitating. Some say he could not swear loyalty to William unless the exiled James Stuart gave his permission. Others claim MacIain was just too damn proud and defiant to give in so easily. Whatever the truth, he waited until 31 December to set off to Fort William to take the oath, but once there was told it could only be taken by the sheriff at Inveraray, 60 miles away. It took MacIain and his party some days to reach the Campbell stronghold in Argyll, battling through biting winds and freezing snow. Even when they arrived there was a delay before he finally pledged his allegiance – six days after the deadline. In Argyll he was assured word would be sent to Edinburgh that the last of the clans had fallen into line and, with letters promising the protection of the Fort William garrison tucked in his sporran, MacIain made his way back to Glencoe. In London and Edinburgh however, Scottish politicians were already planning his death.

Sir John Dalrymple, Master of Stair, was Secretary of State and keen to see the MacDonalds brought to heel. MacIain's delay was used as an excuse by him and Campbell, Lord of Argyll to carry out 'a great work of charity . . . in rooting out that damnable sept, the worst in all the Highlands'. The fact that MacIain *had* actually promised allegiance was ignored.

On 1 February, 60-year-old Captain Robert Campbell of Glenlyon (who had by then lost what was left of his lands through gambling and drink) arrived in Glencoe with 120 of Argyll's men. They were told that there was no room for them in Fort William so they were to be billeted with MacIain's clan. The old chief, bound by the rules of Highland hospitality, had to take the soldiers in. For over ten days the troops ate with the MacDonalds. They slept in their homes. They played games with their children. Captain Campbell drank with MacIain and his sons.

Finally, on 12 February, Captain Campbell received a written order that was to be the death warrant for the MacDonalds. It read,

> You are to put all to the sword under 70. You are to have special care that the old fox and his sons do on no account escape your hands. You are to secure all avenues, that none escape; this you are to put in execution at five o'clock precisely . . .

The orders told him that reinforcements would arrive to help with the massacre. They did not come. Whether this was by accident or design no one knows.

According to tradition, a fire was lit on Signal Rock (which is in the woods about 20 minutes' walk behind the visitors' centre) to mark the beginning of the murders. However, the snow was so heavy that few, if any, of the soldiers would have seen it. What followed, though, was horrific – even by Scottish standards.

MacIain was shot as he rose from his bed, a pistol ball tearing off part of his head. His wife was stripped forcibly, soldiers using their teeth to tear the rings from her fingers. Families were shot or bayoneted, their blood staining the snow scarlet. Children were gunned down as they pleaded for their lives. Families were lined up against dunghills and cut down. Captain Campbell tried to save one man after he found a letter promising these people military protection. Perhaps he realised then what a terrible thing he had ordered, or perhaps he was sickened by his own brutality, but he lowered his sword. Another officer arrived though, and put a musket ball in the man's head. Homes and byres burned red through the snow, cattle and sheep were driven off and everywhere there was the sound of gunfire, screaming and the lamentations of women.

They say that not all the soldiers took part in the killing and that two officers resigned their commissions on the spot. There is a tradition that the Argyll soldiers knew about the orders before that night and that a few tried to warn their hosts. According to one tale, a soldier told a dog within earshot of its owners that if it knew what was good for it, the hound would sleep in the heather that night. Another is said to have told a rock, known as McNeil's Stone, that if it knew what was going to happen that night even it would be up and away. Children listening nearby rushed to tell their parents. By the time the killing stopped, 38 MacDonalds were dead, the rest had managed (or were allowed) to escape into the hills. Some of them died there.

History has blamed the Campbells for the horrors of that February night and to an extent the clan must accept that. Attempts have been made to excuse Captain Campbell for his actions, saying he was only a soldier following orders, but surely that is not good enough. He could have refused to follow them. He could have even stood back and let his men do it. But he took an active part in the massacre – at least until he found that letter.

In London, a journalist got wind of the events in Glencoe and published a pamphlet to bring the atrocity into the public eye. The solids, as they say, hit the air conditioning. King Billy denied reading orders sanctioning the act. The Master of Stair was, eventually, forced to resign but was not kept away long from the corridors of power. Captain Campbell ultimately drank himself to death and was buried in a pauper's grave in Belgium.

There is one particular story worth retelling about this area. A traveller was passing through the glen one dark and snowy night and heard a child crying against the wind. He stopped at a cottage and rapped on the door. An old shepherd appeared and the traveller told him he could hear a child crying as if lost. The old man looked out into the blizzard sadly and nodded.

'Aye,' he said, 'there is a child out there and it cries, sure enough. But there is nothing you can be doing for it, the soul, for it has been crying since long, long ago.'

I drove into Glencoe village in search of the monument to the massacre but as usual there were no signs. I was staying the night here and by then it was dark, so I decided to leave it until morning. The next day, unfortunately (but unsurprisingly) the weather broke. It had been fine all the way up but now the rain struck with stunning ferocity. If it is true that Glencoe receives 90 inches of rain every year, then I think most of it fell on me that day.

I asked the hotel receptionist for the location of the monument and she told me that it would be signposted. I disabused her of that notion immediately, pointing out that it was not the policy in Scotland to signpost these things because we wouldn't want anyone actually to *visit* them, for heaven's sake. As it turned out, the monument was down the one lane I had not tried the previous evening. But of *course* . . .

The Celtic Cross was first erected in 1883 by a direct descendent of MacIain and refurbished by the Clan Donald Land Trust of the USA in 1992, 300 years after the massacre. It sits on a quiet spot on a small hill, with the misty slopes rising behind it. I peered through the rain and the railings at the foot of the cross where visitors have laid wreaths – little wooden crosses, rowan twigs, sprigs of heather and one small white rock with a metal plate inscribed 'ROCK FROM THE GLENCOE CLAN HENDERSON, SAVANNAH, GEORGIA, USA 1991'. Like the flowers and wreaths at Culloden, there was something very touching about all this. American visitors, who often seem to care more about Scottish history and culture than native-born Scots, had left many of these small memorials. It does bear out the saying that the violent deaths and betrayal of trust that night in February so long ago will be remembered as long as the hills stand.

DEVIL'S GALLOP

THIRTY-EIGHT
A Murder in Appin

Near Ballachulish, I paused in the shop of 'Highland Mystery World' (partly to hide from the rain but also to buy a gift for the present Mrs Skelton). This enjoyable attraction deals with Celtic myth and legend, and has actors leading visitors through often dimly-lit sets from which anything can jump out, and invariably does. I first visited the place soon after it had opened and can recommend it without hesitation. It's fun, it's informative and such enterprise should be supported. And if the owner is reading this, that'll be 50 pounds, please.

Ballachulish was well known for its slate mines, the remains of which can still be seen from the small marina. Also visible from here is Eilean Munde, the burial isle of the MacDonalds, Stewarts and Camerons. The island was the final resting place of the murdered MacIain and his wife.

But this was not why I was in Ballachulish. The real reason for stopping here lay hidden by trees at the entrance to the road bridge, which crosses the narrows between Loch Linnhe and Loch Leven. There I found the monument to Seamas a Ghlinne, James of the Glens, a Stewart of Appin who was falsely accused of murder and executed on this spot. Even today, the identity of the real killer is hotly debated – and protected. Waters were further muddied when Robert Louis Stevenson included the killing in *Kidnapped*, using the real names of some of the people involved but drastically changing their characters.

To find the monument, I took the Oban road from the A82 and drove under the bridge to park near the Ballachulish Hotel. I then climbed the steps back up to the opening of the bridge. The large monument is in a copse there, unseen from the road. It was the first of three sites I would visit in connection with the events that make up The Appin Mystery.

The first victim in this celebrated true-life puzzler was Colin Campbell of Glenure who, like many of his kinsmen, was loyal to the Crown during the 1745 uprising. As a reward he was appointed Government Factor to forfeited Stewart and Cameron estates in Appin and Lochaber respectively. Campbell was not the monstrous creature painted by the Jacobites (and to an extent Stevenson). His mother was a Cameron and he was a boyhood friend with James Stewart. Campbell was reasonable and compassionate towards the tenants on the estates – so much so that his masters in London and Edinburgh reprimanded him. 'You're too reasonable and compassionate towards the tenants,' they said. 'Don't you know you're a Campbell and a king's man and you're supposed to be a bit of a bastard?'

One of the tenants to whom he was too reasonable and compassionate was his old chum James of the Glens – who was, in fact, a Jacobite, albeit one who had been pardoned. James was also the collector of funds to support exiled Jacobites, something he did with Campbell's full knowledge. To help his old friend avoid any further pressure from above, James agreed to move to a smaller farm. Campbell, though, felt the need to flex his disciplinary muscles from then on and this put a strain on the friendship. Then, in 1752, another character stepped into the story – Allan Breck Stewart, James's foster-son.

Allan Breck is described as being black-haired, round-shouldered and knock-kneed, with a face bearing the deep craters of a childhood attack of smallpox. His name Breck was derived from the Gaelic 'Breac', which means 'speckled'. He was, in short, a far cry from the actors Peter Finch, Michael Caine, Dan O'Herlihy, David McCallum and Armand Assante, who have all played him. He was nothing like the dashing, romantic figure of the novels and films, being more of a sly, drunken blowhard with decidedly dishonest tendencies. He was not the ardent Jacobite of fiction but had actually begun his military career in General Cope's army, switching sides at Prestonpans, no doubt when he saw the way the battle was going. He was certainly no coward, though. He did remain on the Scottish side and was active after the war in raising recruits for French regiments, which is what brought him back to Appin. It was the real-life Breck who may have led Stevenson to call Colin Campbell the 'Red Fox', for while

Breck was drinking in an inn at Portnacroish further down the coast, he said that he would pay someone to 'bring him the skin of that red fox'. Although Campbell had red hair, he was known locally as 'Red Colin' but never the 'Red Fox'.

By May 1752, Campbell was preparing to evict some tenants who had not sworn their allegiance to the Crown. James Stewart tried to prevent this, but in Edinburgh Baron Kennedy of Dunure told him that the court was not sitting but if somehow he could postpone the evictions legally, then the case could be heard later. James tried to get a lawyer to make a formal protest at the site of the evictions but found it difficult to find one who was willing to upset the Government's Factor.

Meanwhile, Colin Campbell was across Loch Leven in Cameron country collecting rents. There had been rumours that his mother's kin were plotting his murder and he was relieved to climb off the ferry at Ballachulish on 14 May 1752.

'Boy, am I relieved to be climbing off this ferry,' he told his three companions. (Actually, what he said was, 'I am safe now that I am out of my mother's country.' But brother, was he wrong!)

The murderer set off westwards towards Kentallen via the thick forest at Leitir Mhor, on the shoulder of Appin. It was here that a shot rang out and Red Colin slumped from his horse. A man wearing 'dun coloured' clothing and carrying a shoulder gun was seen running away along the side of the hill above the murder scene. Allan Breck was the principal suspect but he was nowhere to be found, although clothing was discovered near to his hideout. That clothing was of a completely different colour from that described by eye-witnesses to the murder, but they did belong to James of the Glens – and the authorities couldn't wait to charge this well-known Jacobite as an accomplice in the murder.

There is no doubt James had nothing to do with the ambush. There was no real evidence on which to hold him, but the authorities not only held him, they also convicted him at a kangaroo court in Inveraray. A Campbell sat on the judging panel and there were a further 11 of the clan in the 15-man jury. A fair trial was not on the cards, especially as the prosecution were willing to overlook facts and present perjured evidence.

DEVIL'S GALLOP 189

A band of Camerons made plans to rescue James from the gallows erected at Cnap a'Chaolais, overlooking Loch Leven and the ferry on which Campbell had crossed that day. But James refused their help, knowing that the soldiers would wreak a terrible revenge on the land and not wishing to bring further pain to his family. And so on 8 November, as the wind raged and the rain lashed at the rocky outcrop (something like the weather on the day I was there), James proclaimed his innocence for the final time and was judicially murdered on the gallows. The body remained there for many months, the flesh rotting and being eaten away by crows. When his bones slid away from the chains that bound them, they were wired together and hanged again.

The skeleton dangled from the chains for three long years until his family was finally allowed to cut it down for burial. The gibbet was torn down and thrown into the loch. When it washed ashore it was reputed to bring bad luck to anyone who touched it but was eventually used by workmen to form part of a gate in Glen Nant.

So who did murder Red Colin Campbell of Glenorchy? Some say it was Allan Breck; others that it was Red Ewan MacColl – who not only possessed 'dun coloured clothing' but whose family also kept the rifle known as the 'Slinneanach', a shoulder gun similar to that carried by the real murderer. A MacColl had actually given perjured evidence too, claiming that James of the Glens had threatened to kill Colin Campbell.

Writer John Prebble believed that it was either Donald Roy or Dugald Roy MacOllonie, a father and son who may have been among those plotting to kill Campbell while he was in Cameron country. Prebble points out (in *John Prebble's Scotland*) that MacOllonie was a suspect in an earlier slaying mirroring that of Red Colin's, when an officer in the Hanoverian militia was shot in a wood by a man hiding in ambush on the side of a hill.

According to local legend, the real identity of the Appin murderer is known to a select few in the Stewart clan. A very helpful woman in Ballachulish's tourist information office told me that at least two people locally know the truth, which is handed down from generation to generation. But they are not talking and never will.

The monument above the bridge on the site of the execution is topped by a lump of stone said to have been from the ruins of James Stewart's farmhouse. I also visited the site of the murder, by following the A828 Oban road, past the Craiglinnhe Guest House, until I neared a house called Craigallen. Amazingly for Scotland, a sign for the Appin Murder Cairn directed me from the road towards a Forestry Commission track. I parked at the foot of it and walked the rest of the way, until another sign pointed off into the trees. (Signs to a point of gruesome interest? In Scotland? Somebody must have been ill!)

The 'Cairn Murt na Hapainn' (to use its Gaelic name) is relatively new. The older, moss-covered marker was removed some years ago, as were most of the old trees that grew around it. Now there is this smaller cairn, no doubt less impressive than the original.

I continued on the A828 through the dampness until a sign for Keil directed me off to the right. It was in a small graveyard here that James's bones were eventually laid to rest beside those of his wife, Margaret. The track led me through a gate to a farmyard. Signs warned me not to enter the farmyard so I parked on a piece of lumpy grass and followed a track through another gate to the shore. On the right, up some stone steps and pointed out by a marker etched helpfully with the initials J.G., were the ruined chapel and graveyard. The brass plaque for Seamus a'Ghlinne, placed there in 1938 by two of his descendents, is on the corner of the right wall as you enter the chapel building – but watch where you're putting your feet; I took a tumble on a horizontal slab made slippery by the rain. (It was quite a dramatic fall – legs akimbo, arms flailing, back slamming onto the ground, air forcibly blasting from my lungs – and for the first time that day I was glad the weather was so dreary that there were no other tourists.) On a clear day this little ruin would be in a dramatic position, with the waters of Loch Linnhe stretching down to Lismore Island and Mull. But this day, the grey waters merely slid into a thick, wet mist.

THIRTY-NINE
Bruce's Revenge

I limped to my car and made my way back to the A828, being careful to close all gates behind me. A few miles later I was above Portnacroish and looking down on the islet of Castle Stalker, once a Stewart stronghold, now privately owned but another in our series of 'Most Photographed Castle in Scotland'. I took my pictures from the vantage point of the road above it, hiding behind a large road sign until I plucked up the courage to dart out and snap away against the rain, which, as luck would have it, was being driven horizontally in my direction.

When the MacDougalls fell out of favour for opposing Robert the Bruce, the castle and lands were given to the Stewarts, who had, as we know, remained faithful. In 1490, Duncan Stewart of Appin offered it to James IV for use as a hunting lodge, hence its Gaelic name 'Caisteal Stalcair' – 'Castle of the Hunter'. Later the Campbells came into possession when during a heavy night of drinking, a Stewart agreed to hand the castle over in return for an eight-oared galley. The next day, as he sipped his morning-after Irn Bru, the Stewart realised he'd been had. The Privy Council agreed with him but the Campbells refused to part with it and there followed a lengthy siege until the Campbells gave up and the Stewarts took possession again. Ownership was then disputed for many years and it passed back and forward until after the Battle of Killiecrankie when the Stewarts, who fought on the winning side, chased the Campbells from the ramparts. There then followed another siege, which lasted a year before once again the Campbells were in control. By the time the 1745 rebellion came around, the castle was reduced to garrisoning King George's troops and after that it fell into ruin. Restoration work began in the 1960s and it is now a private residence.

DEVIL'S GALLOP

There was another battle fought near here and to find its monument I drove into Portnacroish, where I parked outside a row of terraced houses and walked back along the road to the churchyard. I knew there was a monument somewhere there – I'd read about it and a battered sign near the church gate even mentioned it – but I couldn't find it anywhere. Finally, after my tenth circuit of the small churchyard, I chanced to look up to my right and saw the grey finger of stone on a small rise, partially hidden by trees and bushes. I forced my way through the foliage and climbed the rocks until I could read the inscription on the obviously neglected monument. It read:

> Above this spot was fought the bloody battle of Stalc, in which many hundreds fell when the Stewarts and the MacLarens, their allies, in defence of Dugald, chief of Appin, son of Sir John Stewart, lord of Lorne and Innermeath, defeated the combined forces of the MacDougalls and MacFarlanes.

In 1463, at his own wedding in Dunstaffnage Castle, near Oban, Sir John Stewart was murdered by Alan MacDougall. The marriage had made Dougal Stewart the legitimate heir to Castle Stalker, which is what upset MacDougall. Relations after the murder deteriorated to such an extent that a full battle was the only thing likely to clear the air. This happened here in 1468 and during the gory goings-on, Alan MacDougall found himself at the wrong end of a claymore and the Stewart forces emerged victorious.

From Portnacroish, I continued on the A828 until I crossed the Connel Bridge, turning left onto the A85, passing through Taynuilt (near which is Glen Nant, where the workman recycled James of the Glens' gibbet to make a gate) and on through the Pass of Brander. This is dominated by the mighty Ben Cruachan (3,695 feet), so beloved of the Campbells that they used its name as their battle cry. I understand 'Cruachann' is Gaelic for 'thigh' or 'haunch', but I really don't see that striking fear into an enemy. 'Crotch', maybe, 'armpit' certainly, but not 'thigh'. Much of the mountain has been hollowed out, and is used as a power station, which can be toured if that's what lights your candle. However, I was here because this was where Robert the Bruce wreaked his revenge on the MacDougalls for nicking his brooch at Dalrigh.

It was in August 1308 that Bruce felt strong enough to come back into Argyll and take on the MacDougalls again. He and his army were on their way to Dalmally, following roughly the same route as the present road, when Bruce's guerrilla eye realised that the pass was an ideal place for an ambush. Even today you can see why. The rock-strewn sides of the mountain stretch up into the mist on the left, while to the right the waters of the River Awe flow dark and deep. This time Bruce was accompanied by James, the Black Douglas, whom he sent with a group of men up the side of Ben Cruachan.

When the attack came, the MacDougalls promptly found themselves fighting on two sides, a front and a rear, as the Black Douglas lunged at them from above. John of Lorne, watching from a galley on Loch Awe, realised his forces were 'well gubbed' (to use a military term) so he picked up his marbles and went home. Bruce had punished the MacDougalls for their disloyalty but he didn't get his brooch back.

Once through the claustrophobic Pass of Brander, the landscape opens up to reveal the grey expanse of Loch Awe. The road took me down to the village of Loch Awe and a view of Kilchurn Castle. A ferry carries visitors to the castle, which at one time was on an island but floodwaters have receded since then and it is now on a spit of land jutting out into the loch. Nothing of huge importance took place here (apart from it being burned by Cromwell's troops in 1654) but I thought I'd have a look at it from the jetty because the same storm that pulled down the Tay Bridge in 1879 also demolished part of the castle. It is also in a quite incredible location and is, again, one of the 'Most Photographed Castles in Scotland'.

I then headed back to Tyndrum. The mist was rising like smoke from the tree-lined hills while torrents of water cascaded from streams at the roadside. As I neared Tyndrum, I saw the grey waters of Lochan na Bi on the right-hand side of the road just before I reached the junction where earlier I had headed north. Here, it is believed, a battle was fought in 729 between the Pictish King Nechtan and the Irish invader Oengus, son of Fergus, who laid Argyll to waste in later years.

Once in Tyndrum I was back on my old friend the A82, as far as Crianlarich, where I stayed the night. The next day I would be heading back into MacGregor country.

The following morning the weather looked more promising. The rain had disappeared and a watery sun was trying desperately to leak through the clouds. I left my hotel for my first stop, which turned out to be five minutes away, on the A85 through Glen Dochart. Shortly after leaving Crianlarich, with Ben More looming up on the right, a narrow loch can be glimpsed through the trees on the left. This is Loch Dochart and a small wooded island here carries the ruins of a castle, once a Campbell stronghold – until one frozen winter night when a band of hardy MacGregors crept across the ice-covered waters and butchered the lot of them. This was one of the seven castles held by Black Duncan Campbell of Glenorchy and he took it from the McNabs.

A small strip of land separates Loch Dochart from Loch Iubhair, which figures in a somewhat gory tale about the death of the great Celtic hero, Fionn, or Fingal. According to legend, a man called Taileachd, who lived on one of the islands here, had fallen in love with a woman who was of the 'Sidthe', (pronounced 'shee') or fairy folk. Problems arose when Fionn was also smitten by her. To settle the argument, the fairy said that whoever could leap from the island onto the mainland would win her affections. As luck would have it, both men, being mighty warriors, managed the jump. With events at an impasse, it was then decided that they should try the leap backwards. Taileachd pulled it off again but Fionn landed in mud up to his neck. Taileachd then seized the opportunity to cut off his rival's head.

Almost immediately, Taileachd knew he had made a mistake. The Fingalian band made the Mafia look like social workers and by killing their leader he was almost certainly in line for an offer he couldn't refuse. So he rushed off to Loch Laidon on Rannoch Moor, carrying with him Fionn's napper. Fingal's band pursued him but the man had a head start, so to speak. Once on Rannoch, Taileachd realised he was knackered and stuck the head on a pole before setting off for a secret hideout on Ben Alder. When the Fingalians found their leader's head, one of them stuck his finger under his 'Tooth of Knowledge' (as you would). This gave Fionn's head the power of speech and he told his men where the murderer was hiding. They found him in a cave on the mountain where they cut off both his hands, burned out his eyes with boiling beer (of all things) and then stuck their spears through his heart. Something tells me he did not survive such treatment. (Fionn's burial place, by the way, is reputed to be in Killin. It is marked by a curiously shaped standing stone, obviously ignored by the authorities, in a patch of reeds in a field behind the school near to a park.)

I headed onwards from the two lochs, remaining on the A85 and descending steep Glen Ogle, with its kamikaze sheep, who wander across the narrow road with sudden, alarming determination. Across the valley, a railway line holds on tenaciously to the side of the hill, crossing streams and gullies via viaducts. Finally at Lochearnhead the A85 angles off towards Comrie, but I drove straight on, the road now the A84, following signs for Callander and Stirling. My next stop, Balquhidder, was likely to be a lengthy one, for there are many stories to be told – and they are all about the MacGregor clan.

DEVIL'S GALLOP

FORTY
Rob Hood

The first thing I thought when I looked down at Rob Roy MacGregor's grave was that they'd never get Liam Neeson in there unless they folded him twice. I mean the actual area covered by the grave is tiny – especially when you consider that there is apparently more than Red Rob down there. According to the markings on the front of the grave, his wife and a couple of sons are also buried there, although I have been reliably informed that even more MacGregors than that are interred there.

Rob Roy came into the world at Glengyle, at the head of Loch Katrine. An extract from the Register of Baptisms at Buchanan Parish shows he was baptised on 7 March 1671, the third son of Donald MacGregor and Margaret Campbell. Donald fought for Dundee at Killiecrankie, along with Rob's brother John. They were captured and held prisoner in Edinburgh. When the name MacGregor was banned by law, Rob was able to take his mother's name and claim the protection of the Duke of Argyll. In January 1693 he married Mary Helen MacGregor and they had at least three sons – James Mór ('mór' means 'tall'), Coll and Robert, or Robin Oig (Young Rob). They also adopted a cousin, Duncan.

MacGregor received the name Rob Roy (Gaelic: 'Raibert Ruadth' or 'Red Robert') because of his thick, red hair. Another distinguishing feature was his long arms (it is said he could fasten his hose without stooping). This lengthy reach would come in handy during sword fights for he could keep his opponent at bay easily.

Although not a chief as such, Rob Roy did become War Leader of the MacGregors and that entitled him to wear three eagle feathers in his cap. He took part in the Herschip of Kippen, an act of plunder in which, unusually for those days, only one man died. But it was his feud with the Duke of Montrose that turned him into a legend. Rob was an expert drover, taking cattle from their grazing lands in the Highlands to the markets of the Lowlands and into England. Montrose invested in these great drives but after a MacDonald stole much of his cash, Rob found himself destitute and in debt.

James Graham, Duke of Montrose, son of the gallant Marquis, took to the law for recovery of the cash he was owed. He was granted leave to impound Rob Roy's property but his men made the mistake of 'insulting' Rob's wife, Mary (according to the most recent film, she was raped but I don't think things went that far). She and the four boys were forced from their home and out into the harsh winter. From then on, Rob Roy was at war with Montrose. He was supported by the Duke of Argyll, for the feud between the Campbells and the Grahams was still fresh. Rob raided Montrose's cattle and offered other landowners 'blackmail' – protection from theft. It was during this period that he became a Scottish Robin Hood, stealing from the rich (Montrose) to give to the poor (the MacGregors). There are many stories told of his exploits and daring escapes from custody – too many to tell here. One, however, does sum up the spirit of the legend. A MacGregor woman had been unable to pay her twenty pounds rent to Montrose and was to be evicted. Rob Roy heard of this and gave the women the readies, telling her to be sure to obtain a receipt. The woman did so and Rob and his men waited at an inn frequented by the factor. When the man showed up, they relieved him of the rents. Rob had his money back, the woman had proof of payment and Montrose was the loser again. It also didn't harm Rob's P.R. When Argyll was criticised for giving Rob 'wood, water and a roof' (actually a house near Inveraray) the wily Duke replied that Montrose was even more magnanimous – after all, he supplied the man with beef on the hoof, for free.

Rob Roy led his men to the battlefield of Sheriffmuir but remained neutral. Although probably a Jacobite in spirit, he owed a great deal to Argyll, who fought on the Royalist side. So Rob and his men stood back and watched while the battle ebbed and flowed (See Rebel March). When it was over, they descended to the battlefield and robbed the dead. This is perhaps the least attractive side of one of Scotland's heroes, but attitudes were different then. He came out to

DEVIL'S GALLOP

fight again for the Stuarts in 1719 but was captured by General Wade. His luck again held when he was pardoned, and he retired to his home in Balquhidder, where on 28 December 1734, he confounded his enemies once more by dying in bed.

His son, Robin Oig, was not so lucky. He does not appear to have been the perfect answer to a fair maiden's prayer, being described as, 'a tall lad, thin, pale-coloured, squint-eyed, brown haired, pock-pitted, ill-legged, in-kneed and broad-fitted'. At the age of 20 he was accused of shooting a MacLaren with his father's gun after an argument over land. He went on the run, joined the army and was wounded at the Battle of Fontenoy. He was accused 17 years later of abducting a young widow and went to the gallows in Edinburgh. Lovers of Stevenson's *Kidnapped* will recall that it was Robin Oig who beat Allan Breck in the piping contest somewhere on the Braes of Balquhidder. 'Ye have mair music in your sporran than I have in my head,' said Breck generously, prompting me to wonder if Robin had a personal CD player tucked away in his pouch.

Behind the grave of Rob and his family lie the ruins of the old church (the new one is a few yards up the hill). It was here, towards the end of the sixteenth century, that a MacGregor chief made a bizarre pledge over the decapitated head of a murdered Drummond.

A group of MacGregors were on their way home through the royal forest of Glen Artney when they made the mistake of killing a deer. As anyone who has seen any of the *Robin Hood* films knows, slaughtering royal venison without permission is a big no-no – as these MacGregors soon learned, for they were caught by the king's forester, a Drummond, who without further ado had their ears cut off. The men were then sent home as a warning to any other raiding MacGregors.

As we now know, the Clan MacGregor was not the sort to let such an insult lie and revenge was sworn. Some time later they ambushed the king's forester and cut off his head. With their trophy wrapped in a plaid, they began to make their way back to Balquhidder. On the way they stopped at the home of Stewart of Ardvorlich, who had married the forester's daughter. The laird was not at home but his wife, showing good Highland hospitality, invited the MacGregors in, completely unaware of what they had in their tartan bundle. She placed bread, cheese and oat cakes on the table for them, and left the room. When she returned, she was faced with a gang of giggling Highlanders and the head of her father sitting on the table, some bread and cheese thrust into his open mouth. Stunned by this lesson in how to get a head without really trying, she ran from the house, her shrieks echoing from the hills.

When her husband returned he found the house empty. The MacGregors had long since left for their homes in Balquhidder. The weeks passed and there was still no sign of his wife, although there were stories from outlying crofts of a strange, mad woman living in the hills. The Stewart tracked this woman down and found it was his wife. Although she was indeed quite mad, she was able to tell him what had happened.

The band of murderers had already told their chief, Alasdair of Glenstrae, what they had done. He took Drummond's head from them and placed it on the altar of the old church. Laying both hands on the gory prize, Glenstrae pledged to protect with his life the men who had committed the killing. He then bid the other men of the clan to do the same.

But Stewart of Ardvorlich was not put off by the MacGregor stand. He was granted a letter of 'Fire and Sword' against them and in 1590 he and Lord Drummond came to the Braes of Balquhidder in force and summarily executed 12 MacGregors.

DEVIL'S GALLOP

FORTY-ONE
Fairy Story

From Balquhidder, I followed the winding road back to the A84 and once again headed for Aberfoyle. The scenery here is simply marvellous, even compared to the other breathtaking vistas I saw on this particular trip. Just before Callander I passed Ben Ledi, near the summit of which is the Lochan nan Corp, the 'Small Lake of the Dead Bodies'. It was here that a large group of Highlanders (mainly of the Clan Kessanach according to legend) fell through the ice and drowned while heading from Glen Finglass to a funeral. So many people died during this tragedy that the name Kessenach died out.

I turned right before Callander to head for Aberfoyle. The road (the A821) took me alongside Loch Venachar and Loch Achray, which lie under the shadow of Ben An. Again, everywhere I looked was like a picture postcard. As I reached the edge of Loch Achray, though, just as the road cuts off towards Loch Katrine, storm clouds were starting to gather and I knew I was in for another downpour. The rain stayed off, though, as I drove through the Duke's Pass and the Achray forest, allowing me to appreciate even more incredible scenery. Autumn was beginning to burst through and the trees were turning in a riot of browns, greens and golds, punctuated here and there by flashes of blue water.

The torrent hit as I reached Aberfoyle and was following a side road to Doune Hill. The rain drummed on the car and I wondered if I *really* needed to make the climb up the hill to see the fairy tree. But in the end, I forced myself to don my wet-weather gear, shoulder my camera bag and set out through the monsoon.

The story I was here to investigate concerned one Robert Kirk – a seventh son, a circumstance which according to Highland lore puts him in touch with all sorts of supernatural odds and ends. He was minister of Balquhidder for a time but it was while he was minister at Aberfoyle that he wrote a book called *The Secret Commonwealth*, or to use its catchy subtitle:

> an essay of the Nature and Actions of Subterranean (and, for the most part) Invisible People heretofor going under the name of Elves, Faunes and Fairies, or the lyke among the Low country Scots, as they are described by those who have the SECOND SIGHT: and now, to occasion further inquiry, collected and compared, by a Circumspect Inquirier residing among the Scottish-Irish in Scotland.

According to legend, Kirk gave away so many of the Sidthe secrets that they punished him by stealing his soul and locking it away forever in a large pine tree at the top of the hill here. His body was buried in the old churchyard, which lies between the hill and Aberfoyle, but the vengeful Sidthe even took that, replacing it with a 'stock' – a sort of fairy doppelganger. As I splashed towards the foot of the hill I wished they had imprisoned him in a tree further down. But that's fairies for you: no consideration.

Just before I diverted from the wide path to make my ascent up a hillside track, I saw a sign that told me the area was a training ground for huskies. I hoped a team would happen by and give me a pull. I could hear no tell-tale cries of 'mush' though, so I stepped onto the narrow dirt trail and began to wade upstream. Battling against the elements made the climb seem longer than it actually was, but finally I made it. Just as I reached the clearing on the summit, a miracle occurred – the rain stopped and the sun came out, its rays streaming through the branches with such intensity that I thought I'd wandered into a Ridley Scott movie. This feeling of unreality was heightened by the scene before me – for surrounding the giant tree were hundreds of rags and paper streamers, left there by people anxious to have their wishes granted by the fairy folk. They dangled from twigs and branches all around, although not on the fairy tree itself. It was a sight that made the trek, and squelching feet, well worth it.

After taking some pictures, I stopped to look at some of the wishes. I soon discovered that it was not just children who believed in fairies

DEVIL'S GALLOP

for some wishes were obviously adult in sentiment. People wanted promises kept, wishes granted and one longed for world peace (clearly left by a beauty queen). I recorded some of them but, amazingly, my mini tape-machine failed me just at this point. It had been working fine at the foot of the hill, and it worked again later but it *refused* to work here. There was either something decidedly spooky on that hilltop or the rain had got to it.

I spent some time at the fairy tree, for there was an incredible feeling of peace at this spot – even if Robert Kirk was perhaps hammering away from the inside the tree. On my way back down I met a young couple on their way uphill with their son, who couldn't have been any more than five.

'Hello,' he said as I stepped off the path to let them past.

'Hello yourself,' I replied.

'It's very muddy,' he opined.

'That it is,' I said. His father smiled wanly and asked how far it was to the top. I told him that it wasn't far and walked on before turning again and shouting after them, 'But it's worth it!'

And it was.

Returning through Aberfoyle, I started my last trip home to Glasgow. I diverted only once, when I saw a sign for the Lake of Menteith. Inchmahome Priory lies on an island in the middle of this, the only 'lake' in Scotland. Little Mary Stuart, later to be Queen of Scots, was spirited here from Stirling Castle after the disastrous Battle of Pinkie. She hid here for some time, learning some Spanish and Latin, as well as the native French tongue of her mother, Mary of Guise. Eventually, as the English closed in, she was smuggled to Dumbarton Rock and then off to France. She was only five years old. Thirteen years later she would return, already a widow, and would embark on the rest of the adventure that was her reign.

The island can be reached by boat and is studded with chestnut trees (the seeds for which came from Rome). Parts of the ruins are naturally strongly associated with Mary but there is also a 'Nun's Hill'. It was here that a nun from the priory was buried in an upright position as punishment for her sins. She had fallen in love with a clan chief and they had planned to elope. He was called away, though, to some battle or other where he was mortally wounded. Before he died he confessed his love for the nun to a monk, who journeyed to the island and waited for the nun to appear at the lovers' meeting place. And there he drowned her, as a punishment for betraying her vows. Christian charity clearly never entered his heart. The Covenanters would have loved him.

And why is this the only lake in Scotland? One explanation puts it down to the Earl of Menteith's betrayal of William Wallace at Robroyston in Glasgow, when he turned over the bannock as a signal to the waiting English troops. Because he was working for Edward, it was decided that the English word 'lake' should be used on the stretch of water bearing his name, rather than the Scottish 'loch'.

It's probably not true, but it's good enough for me.

Select Bibliography

Adam, J. (ed), *The Declaration of Arbroath* (Herald Press, 1993)

Adams, N., *Scotland's Chronicles of Blood* (Robert Hale, 1996)

Alexander, M., *British Folklore, Myths and Legends* (Weidenfeld and Nicolson, 1982)

Andrew, K., *Ayrshire, Kyle and Carrick District* (Alloway Publishing, 1991)

Anonymous, *Scottish Battles* (Lang Syne, 1985)

Balfour, M., *Mysterious Scotland* (Mainstream Publishing, 1997)

Barnett, T.R., *The Road to Rannoch and the Summer Isles* (Robert Grant and Sons, 1924)

Barnett, T.R, *Border By-Ways and Lothian Lore* (John Grant, 1925)

Bell, J.J., *The Glory of Scotland* (Harrap, 1932)

Blair, A., *Tales of Ayrshire* (Shepheard-Walwyn, 1983)

Bord, J. & C., *Ancient Mysteries of Britain* (Grafton Books, 1986)

Boyle, A., *Ayrshire Heritage* (Alloway Publishing, 1990)

Burke, G., *Take the High Road* (Lang Syne, 1989)

Campbell, M., *Strange Stories of Glasgow and the Clyde* (Lang Syne, 1989)

Castle, J., *Ayr Memories* (Kyle and Carrick District Council, 1994)

Cheetham, J.K., *On the Trail of Mary Queen of Scots* (Luath Press, 1999)

Cowan, I.B., *Ayrshire Abbeys* (Ayrshire Archaeological and Natural History Society, 1986)

Crichton, J.; Guthrie, L.; Hendry, A.; Moffat, W.; Smith, J.H.F., *The Presbytery of Ayr 1581–1981* (Presbytery of Ayr, 1981)

Cuthbertson, D.C., *Carrick Days* (Grant & Murray, 1933)

Deen, R., *On the Trail of Sawney Beane and his Cannibal Family* (Ron Deen, 1995)

Douglas, H., *Portrait of the Burns Country* (Robert Hale, 1968)

Fraser, D., *Discovering East Scotland* (Standard Press, 1974)

Fraser, G.M., *The Steel Bonnets* (Pan, 1974)

Gordon, S., *Highways and Byways in the Central Highlands* (Birlinn, 1995)

Hale, R.B., *The Beloved St Mungo, Founder of Glasgow* (University of Ottawa, 1989)

Horan, M., *Scottish Executions, Assassinations and Murders* (Chambers, 1990)

Kermack, W.R., *The Scottish Borders* (Johnston & Bacon, 1967)

Lindsay, M. (ed), *Scotland, an Anthology* (Robert Hale, 1974)

Livingstone, S., *Confess and Be Hanged* (Birlinn, 2000)

Love, D., *The Auld Inns of Scotland* (Robert Hale, 1997)

Love, D., *Pictorial History of Ayr* (Alloway Publishing, 1995)

Love, D., *Scottish Covenanter Stories* (Neil Wilson Publishing, 2000)

Love, D., *Scottish Kirkyards* (Robert Hale, 1989)

MacGregor, F., *Famous Scots* (Gordon Wright, 1984)

Mackay, G., *Scottish Place Names* (Lomond, 2000)

Mackay, J.; Livingstone, A., *Tales of Rob Roy, Loch Lomond, Stirling and the Trossachs* (Lang Syne, 1982)

McKean, C., *The District of Moray* (Scottish Academic Press, 1987)

MacLean, F., *Highlanders, a History of the Clans* (David Campbell Publishers, 1995)

McNeill, P., *Prestonpans and Vicinity* (1902)

Marsden, J., *Alba of the Ravens* (Constable, 1997)

Mitchell, A. (ed), *Pre-1855 Gravestones and Inscriptions, an Index for Carrick, Ayrshire* (Scottish Genealogy Society, 1988)

Morton, H.V., *In Search of Scotland* (Methuen, 1929)

Paul, Sir J.B. (ed), *The Scots Peerage* (David Douglas, 1905)

Platt, W. S., *Folktales of the Scottish Borders* (Senate, 1999)

Prebble, J., *Culloden* (Penguin, 1996)

Prebble, J., *Glencoe* (Penguin, 1968)

Prebble, J., *John Prebble's Scotland* (Penguin 1986)

Prebble, J., *The Lion in the North* (Secker and Warburg, 1971)

Reese, P., *The Scottish Commander* (Canongate, 1999)

Robertson, W., *Historical Tales and Legends of Ayrshire* (Hamilton, Adams and Co., 1889)

Robertson, W., *Old Ayrshire Days* (John Menzies and Co., 1905)

Ross, D.R., *On the Trail of William Wallace* (Luath Press, 1999)

Ross, D.R., *On the Trail of Robert the Bruce* (Luath Press, 1999)

DEVIL'S GALLOP

Sadler, J., *Scottish Battles* (Canongate, 1996)

Simpson, W.D., *The Highlands of Scotland* (Robert Hale, 1976)

Smith, R., *Catastrophes and Disasters* (Chambers, 1992)

Strawhorn, J., *Ayrshire, the Story of a Coast* (Ayrshire Archaeological and Natural History Society, 1975)

Ure, J., *A Bird on a Wing* (Constable, 1992)

Various, *Discover Scotland* (four volume partwork)

Westwood, J., *Albion, a Guide to Legendary Britain* (Granada, 1985)

Williams, R., *Montrose, Cavalier in Mourning* (Barrie and Jenkins)

Wilson, A.J.; Brogan, D.; McGrail, F., *Ghostly Tales and Sinister Stories of Old Edinburgh* (Mainstream Publishing, 1991)

Wood, J.M., *Witchcraft in South-West Scotland* (EP Publishing Ltd, 1975)

Young, A. & Stead, M.J., *In the Footsteps of Robert the Bruce* (Sutton Publishing, 1999)

Young, A.F., *Encyclopaedia of Scotish Executions 1750–1967* (Eric Dobby Publishers Ltd, 1998)